S0-AJX-945

The
Mahler Symphonies

Unlocking the Masters Series, No. 2

Series Editor
Robert Levine

The
Mahler Symphonies

An Owner's Manual

David Hurwitz

**AMADEUS
PRESS**

Pompton Plains, NJ • Cambridge, UK

Copyright © 2004 by David Hurwitz

All rights reserved. No part of this book may be reproduced in any form, except by a newspaper or magazine reviewer who wishes to quote brief passages in connection with a review.

Published in 2004 by

Amadeus Press, LLC
512 Newark Pompton Turnpike
Pompton Plains, New Jersey 07444, USA

Amadeus Press
2 Station Road
Swavesey, Cambridge CB4 5QJ, UK

For sales, please contact

NORTH AMERICA

AMADEUS PRESS, LLC
c/o Hal Leonard Corp.
7777 West Bluemound Road
Milwaukee, Wisconsin 53213, USA
Tel. 800-637-2852
Fax 414-774-3259

UNITED KINGDOM AND EUROPE

AMADEUS PRESS
2 Station Road
Swavesey, Cambridge CB4 5QJ, UK
Tel. 01954-232959
Fax 01954-206040

E-mail: orders@amadeuspress.com
Website: www.amadeuspress.com

Printed in the United States of America

Library of Congress Cataloging-in-Publication Data

Hurwitz, David, 1961–
The Mahler symphonies : an owner's manual / by David Hurwitz.
    p. cm. — (Unlocking the masters series ; no. 2)
    ISBN 1-57467-099-9
        1. Mahler, Gustav, 1860–1911. Symphonies. 2. Mahler, Gustav, 1860–1911. Lied von der Erde. 3. Symphonies—Analysis, appreciation. I. Title. II. Series.

ML410.M23H86 2004
784.2'184'092—dc22
                                                                          2004018845

To my parents, Dale and Lewis Hurwitz,
who were understandably worried at the odd spectacle
of a thirteen-year-old fixated on Mahler's symphonies,
but who nevertheless let nature take its course

Contents

Acknowledgments

I want to thank everyone at Amadeus Press who contributed to the final shape and design of this book, but especially Bob Levine, who is not only an expert editor and obsessive perfectionist, but a real *Mensch* as well—a rare and truly priceless combination.

Introduction

Listening to Mahler

This is a book about listening to Gustav Mahler's music, which is not the same thing as a book about Mahler. The difference is important. Mahler (1860–1911) was a fascinating character, the greatest conductor of his age, hugely gifted, possessed of a larger-than-life personality. He lived at a time of tremendous artistic and intellectual ferment, the triumph and tragedy of his personal and professional life set against the decline of the Hapsburg Empire and the collapse of the old European order that would culminate in the horrors of the First World War. He consulted Sigmund Freud about his marital problems and counted among his friends and acquaintances many of the leading artists and intellectuals of his age. The story of his life makes for titillating reading, and it's been done many times.

This book, however, is about the experience of hearing music; about what you as a listener are going to encounter if you take the time to sit down, either at home or in concert, and immerse yourself in one of Mahler's extraordinary compositions. This is not "Mahler for Dummies." "Dummies" aren't interested in Mahler's music, and they certainly wouldn't be willing to spend any time getting to know it. Equally, this is not "Mahler for Mahlerites," those odd fanatics who dwell on such trivia as what the great man had for dessert on May 26,

1902, and what effect this may have had on the viola part in measure 462 of Symphony No. 5. The only extra-musical facts to be considered are those that have a direct bearing on what you will hear. Similarly, you won't find comments by Mahler's contemporaries, or even his own remarks, quoted at length, for the simple reason that what he said about his music really has nothing to do with what you, as the listener, think or feel when you hear it. I am starting from the simple assumption that when going to a concert or purchasing a recording, you will want to sit down and listen with nothing more than useful suggestions on how to get the most out of the immediate experience of the music itself.

The obvious way to accomplish this particular goal is to discuss each major work individually, and I will do just that. After the discussions of the ten completed symphonies, I also offer two appendices: (1) an in-depth discussion of Mahler's use of the orchestra keyed to some of the music included on your sample CD, and (2) "The Symphonies at a Glance": a subjectively chosen series of tables that identify some especially "Mahlerian" musical features and show how they are distributed among the movements of the individual works.

There's nothing in this book that requires you to adopt a systematic or straight-line approach, and although the various essays do make limited reference to each other, you can jump in anywhere you want and browse as suits your fancy. In fact, just as you would not listen to all of Mahler's symphonies in a row, I would not suggest that you read these essays at a sitting. They presuppose a fresh experience of the music, and no detailed description will make much sense if you haven't heard the work in question.

Regarding the incomplete Tenth Symphony, it pains me not to give it consideration here, but after much thought (and despite its containing—see appendix 2 for details—one of

Mahler's juiciest instrumental screams and most primal thuds), I have concluded that none of the extant attempts at completion offers enough information to permit a thorough discussion of what Mahler's ultimate intentions were, particularly as regards orchestration. The best edition remains Deryck Cooke's, and if you decide to try it, you will find that these essays will arm you with all of the tools that you need to decide just how much Mahler there is in it.

Finally, I also want to draw the distinction between *descriptions* (which the following essays are) and *analyses* (which they most definitely are not). This difference is important and rather like the difference, when you buy a new household appliance or piece of machinery, between reading an owner's manual to learn how to use it and needing to know how to build one yourself. No composer expects his listeners to know *how* he does what he does, but it can be very useful to understand *what* it is that he does. That is exactly what I propose to offer.

The
Mahler Symphonies

Symphony No. 1

Scoring:

- four flutes, two players alternating with two piccolos
- four oboes, one player alternating on English horn
- two clarinets in B-flat, A, and C
- one E-flat clarinet alternating on third clarinet in A and bass clarinet in B-flat
- three bassoons, one player alternating on contrabassoon
- seven horns
- five trumpets
- four trombones
- tuba
- harp
- two sets of timpani
- bass drum
- crash cymbals
- suspended cymbal
- bass drum with cymbal attached
- tam-tam
- triangle
- strings (first and second violins, violas, cellos and basses)
- In the finale, Mahler also asks that the first trumpet and E-flat clarinet be doubled in all fortissimo (very loud) passages.

This work, composed between 1884 and 1888, ranks along with the Symphonie fantastique of Berlioz as one of the most remarkable first symphonies by any musician. You will probably find this statement far more useful in listening than the fact that the piece originally had a nickname, "Titan," after a novel by German author Jean Paul. Have you have read Titan by Jean Paul? I haven't, and I have no plans to. And it will really make you feel better to learn that 99.9% of all of those very smart musical scholars who point out this nickname in their program and booklet notes so as to imply that they actually have read it (and therefore intimidatingly let you assume that they know something important that you don't) actually haven't bothered either. After all, why read a tedious early nineteenth-century German novel that no one cares about today (even in Germany) when you can listen to Mahler's First Symphony instead?

First Movement

Before beginning, it is necessary to deal with the issue of sonata form in Mahler, because as you get started on your journey through the symphonies, you will find it a subject of constant discussion in program and CD booklet notes. The term sonata form basically means this: a movement organized on a consistent tonal plan, where the key in which the music begins becomes a sort of musical home base. Initial themes or groups of themes appear in the home key, with contrasting material presented in subsidiary keys (the exposition). These themes and motives (musical figures or patterns) undergo a process of metamorphosis in a development section, which may also introduce new material and is often very dramatic, taking the music through many different keys and leading eventually to a recapitulation, in which all of the original material returns in the home key.

A final wrap-up, or coda, whether loud or soft, usually brings the movement to a close and may include even more development before the final assertion of the primacy of the tonic (the musical term for the home key).

The most important organizational fact about any sonata movement is that what matters is not so much the actual tunes or motives themselves, but rather how much time the music spends getting away from the tonic and getting back again. It is this process that gives the form such versatility and that makes it dramatic: the thematic material is going to go somewhere (musically speaking) and undergo change in the course of its adventures around the tonal universe, while the act of moving (or modulating) from one key to another necessarily involves the accumulation and release of musical tension, making the thematic material active, like characters in a story.

One of the things that makes Mahler's music so original is his willingness to build his works around materials, such as "low class" popular music and natural sounds, that had never been subjected to symphonic treatment before. It therefore follows that his approach to form is as undoctrinaire as his choice of musical themes and motives. The first movement of Mahler's very First Symphony is a nightmare for the fans of the sonata form school of musical analysis, because although there is an exposition of sorts, and Mahler even directs that it be repeated (as often happens in symphonies of the classical period), the music spends almost all of its time in the home key, and absolutely nothing dramatic happens until the very end. Annoying though this may be from the academic perspective, it makes a wonderfully fresh-sounding opening movement to Mahler's First Symphony. In fact, the easiest way to enjoy this movement in dealing with the issue of its form is to think of it as the introduction to the entire work.

The music begins at dawn: the entire string section plays the note A, from the very top of the violins down to the lowest octave of the basses. Against this "sound of silence," woodwinds emit one of Mahler's primal nature motives, only two notes long. Each entrance is scored differently. First you hear piccolo, oboe, and two clarinets; then two flutes, English horn, and bass clarinet; then one oboe and two bassoons turn the two note phrase into a six-note phrase; and then, suddenly, the two clarinets and bass clarinet emit a jolly fanfare in a quicker tempo. Two oboes respond lazily. The six-note phrase returns (with a seventh note added for completion), now played by piccolo, oboe, English horn, and bass clarinet. Then the fanfare returns on three offstage trumpets, answered by the two-note motive speeded up into a little cuckoo call.

Don't worry. I'm not going to take this music a single bar at a time. My point is simply to describe how Mahler's orchestral habits and fingerprints aren't theoretical observations gleaned from years of score study, but simply easily audible facts that you can hear for yourself from the outset: the ever-changing tone colors, nature sounds in the woodwinds, the use of a large and varied assortment of instruments at a quiet dynamic level, the fanfares both onstage and off, the emphasis on wind instruments rather than strings—it's all here in this opening sixty seconds of music, and it's completely original to Mahler.

And so the introduction continues its hypnotic unfolding of tiny events, eventually adding a nostalgic horn duet to the wind phrases and trumpet fanfares. A soft rumble from the timpani introduces softly wandering strings while muted horns take over those six-note woodwind phrases, and ever so gradually the tempo increases, until the fast version of the two-note motive becomes the opening of the cello tune that introduces what passes for the movement's exposition.

There are two things that you should know about this tune. First, it's an actual song (No. 2 in Mahler's Songs of a Wayfarer), with the title "Over the Fields I Went at Morning," so it is clear even from the title just what moods the music is supposed to express—and incidentally, as if any more evidence were needed, the entire point of the introduction. Dawn indeed! Second, pay particular attention not just to the tune but to the soft counter-melody in bass clarinet that plays off it simultaneously as well. Here is a classic case of Mahler's special brand of counterpoint, giving every part independent melodic life. For the next couple of minutes, the music gets increasingly lively, until it reaches a climax decorated by timpani and triangle, quickly subsiding back into the mood of the introduction. Most performances then repeat this whole section, as Mahler suggests.

Once the music settles down again, it's back to the introduction, only this time with little bits of cello tune tossed in. The tuba enters very quietly along with solo bass drum, giving us our very first "Mahlerian thud." A soft timpani roll introduces that wandering string theme from the introduction, only now it's played on the low notes of the harp, a sound that simply didn't exist in the orchestra before Mahler discovered it. Bits of tunes on muted horns join the music's lazy progress, and the mood gradually brightens, leading to a soft horn fanfare that is entirely new and that initiates the recapitulation—essentially, an extended development of "Over the Fields I Went at Morning," presented in a myriad of shifting tonal and instrumental orches-tral colors.

Gradually the mood mellows, then darkens, as against softly thudding strokes of the bass drum, the trumpet fanfares from the introduction blare forth, announcing an impending onslaught. The orchestra gathers itself in a huge crescendo, and with a crash on the cymbals and more heraldic trumpet fanfares, the horns and trombones grandly intone the formerly quiet horn fanfare that was just heard introducing the recapitulation.

From this point on, the music returns to "Over the Fields I Went at Morning," with increasing wildness until the little two-note nature motive becomes Mahler's symbol of rejoicing: jubilantly pounding timpani, which bang the movement to an emphatic and amusing close—funny because timpani and orchestra can't seem to decide who should play first. As I noted earlier, the essential point of this movement's form is that nothing happens until the big climax at the end, but isn't it amazing how entertaining that "nothing" has been?

Second Movement

This rustic peasant dance is the only scherzo (which means "joke," incidentally, but usually consists of a relatively quick dance-style movement in triple time) in all of Mahler's symphonies that has no element of parody or irony. The catchy tunes, bagpipe imitations, and rustic repeated notes on the stopped horns all contribute to the music's gutsy, primitive character. A full stop leads to the middle section (called a trio for various historical and traditional reasons), a svelte tune with lots of sexy string portamento (sliding between notes) and a healthy dose of our composer's favorite "Mahler rhythm" (dum, dadum).

This rhythm has the wonderful quality of being as common to triple-time dance music as to marches in duple-time, a fact which you can be sure was not lost on Mahler when he, for whatever reason, claimed it for his own. The violins get most of the work here, in contrast to the Scherzo's outer sections, where once again, the woodwinds lead. A short transition on solo horn leads back to the opening, more fully scored and drastically shortened, so as to lead to an even more brilliant climax, capped by cymbals, trilling trumpets, and a boisterous final crash.

Third Movement (CD Track 1)

This is the sort of music that got Mahler into trouble in his own day and has proven so fascinating to subsequent generations of listeners. If anything can be said to have "polluted" nearly a century of Holy German Symphonic Purity, then this movement represents a veritable musical Love Canal. The tune is "Frère Jacques" ("Bruder Martin" in German), set in a creepy minor key. The first sounds that are heard, a muted solo double bass over softly thudding muted timpani, actually have their textural origins in Verdi's Rigoletto (Act I, Scene 2). The instruments play the music in a round (the musical term is canon), just as children still sing it today, and the order in which the instruments enter is: solo bass, solo bassoon, muted cellos, solo tuba, solo clarinet, muted violas, solo horn, low flutes (accompanied by soft strokes on the tam-tam), and then groups of winds and strings, leading finally to solo harp in its lower register.

Mahler directs that no matter how many instruments play, the volume must remain very low and without crescendo. You may also notice that the "Frère Jacques" tune, especially when played on the harp, bears a close family resemblance to that wandering string theme at the end of the first movement's introduction. Meanwhile, on top of all of this (0:59), the woodwinds, led by the oboes, chirp out a nose-thumbing little tune containing the Mahler rhythm, like someone trying to look serious at a funeral while failing to conceal a bad case of the hiccups. Sleazy, isn't it?

The round slowly winds down as the harp finishes the main tune, while the thudding timpani and quiet tam-tam keep up the slow march tempo. And then the fun really begins. Two oboes accompanied by wailing trumpets start a klezmerlike melody straight out of Mahler's Czech/Jewish heritage (2:05). This swings gently into a jolly little pub ditty, complete with "Salvation Army" percussion (the boom-chick of bass drum with attached cymbal) and accompanied by violins clicking the strings with the wooden backs of their bows (col legno).

The Jewish music returns (2:43), with the drinking song capped by a wonderful shriek in the violins (like someone grabbing the barmaid's bottom), and then the timpani of the opening interrupt (3:35), funeral march in tow. As this procession marches to its quiet close, low flutes and harp begin a rippling accompaniment (4:50), and in steals what sounds like the most beautiful tune in the world. It comes from another of Mahler's Songs of a Wayfarer, and the music describes the wandering lad going to sleep under a tree at the side of the road. Before that, the same melody was featured in Mahler's early cantata Das Klagende Lied (The Song of Lamentation), where it describes a young man going to sleep in the woods just before his brother murders him to steal a rare flower that will win him the hand in marriage of the queen. This is one of those Mahlerian oases of peace, made all the more gripping by appearing in such lurid surroundings.

Reality returns in the form of the Mahlerian thud on bass drum and tam-tam (6:28). This leads back to "Frère Jacques" and a new counterpoint on the trumpets (7:24) after the "hiccup" theme (scored differently than on its first appearance). The drinking song interrupts obnoxiously, without the Jewish music to introduce it, and with an extra touch of flatulence from the tuba and trombones. The orchestra responds (7:58) with some very strange-sounding whimpers (Mahler asking the violins to actually make squeaking noises by stroking the strings with the wooden back of the bow); the funeral march attempts to intrude, but the clarinets won't have any of that and squeal grotesquely, jerking the orchestra back for one more brief shot of dance music before the violins, accompanied by alternating strokes on suspended cymbals and tam-tam, begin a long, gradual diminuendo that closes the movement more or less as it began, with the sounds of timpani, tam-tam, and finally, two widely spaced, very quiet thuds on the bass drum.

Fourth Movement

Here is a completely accurate verbal description of the opening of Mahler's finale: CRASH! SCREAM! THUD! One of the more entertaining facts about Mahler's approach to writing loud is that he spreads out his noise sequentially. Most composers would have had cymbals, bass drum, timpani, and the dissonant shriek that begin the movement all playing together, but Mahler discovered that it's much more effective to give each a split second to register solo. The orchestration of this opening chord demonstrates the effectiveness of muted trumpets (four) and stopped horns (seven) played very loudly. Their nasty timbre gives the music tremendous bite without covering the squealing woodwinds. So even when Mahler is doing his very best to make a hellish din, his textures retain their characteristic clarity.

The music of this opening is simply the most violent piece of orchestral writing ever conceived up to that time, making even Tchaikovsky's most hysterical climaxes sound a bit tame by comparison. Wild runs in the strings lead to a maniacal brass proclamation (accompanied by cruel four-note descending musical sneers in woodwinds, strings, and muted trumpets with stopped horns), followed by crushing thuds from the bass drum and heavy brass. More rushing strings and brass fanfares introduce a shuddering figure for violins over a crescendo on suspended cymbal, in fact, another motive from the cantata Das Klagende Lied, where it is set to a single word: "Woe!" Gradually all of this commotion leads to an actual theme based on the rhythm of that initial brass proclamation, and if you have a really good memory, you may also recall hearing the opening of this very same theme introduce the big climax in the first movement as well.

This very long melody accumulates so much energy that the only way to stop it is to quite literally pull on its musical reins, an auditory impression accomplished by abrupt suspended cymbal and timpani crescendos cut off by bass drum thwacks, gradually diminishing in strength.

A few more four-note cackles from the brass lead to the lyrical second theme, another very long (several minutes), but this time very pretty, song in the ripest late romantic style. After a passionate climax, the mood turns peaceful, as a hint of the first-movement introduction returns, and then the scene darkens. The violins play metallic-sounding soft tremolos on the bridges of their instruments, while the muted trumpets steal in with their four-note sneer. A sudden crescendo, and the music of the opening returns, with a crash on the cymbal answered by a thud from tam-tam and bass drum. At the height of the tumult, the sound of the orchestra suddenly recedes into the distance, and a hopeful chorale appears on the muted brass (the opening notes are the same as the loud proclamation that opened the movement, only in a bright major key). Then it's back to chaos and violence as all of the music from the opening minute or so returns, leading via horn fanfares to a loud version of the triumphant chorale headed for what looks like victory.

Not quite: what occurs instead is the first of Mahler's "climaxes gone wrong." The music quite literally overshoots its target, and the resultant triumphant tune on the horns, which is nothing more than that original six-note phrase from the first movement with a little two-note tag at the end, slowly fades back into the introductory music from which it came. As fragments of themes from the first movement return, like sad memories, the finale's second theme slowly creeps in, piece by piece, until it rises to one last big climax with cymbal crash.

As this last eruption calms down, the violas wrench the music around with a musical jerk, and the violent textures return. Only now, having been infected with the memory of the first movement, the orchestra arrives at exactly the same approach to the climax that occurred over half an hour ago. Quiet thuds on bass drum and trumpet fanfares, all subtly enriched and amplified compared to their first appearance, lead to the big cymbal crash with heraldic trumpets and horns riding to the rescue, only this time they introduce the triumphant chorale that previously missed the target.

Now its aim is accurate, and to joyously pounding timpani, that six-note phrase from the very beginning of the first movement fulfills its predestined role as victorious conqueror, blasted out by horns that Mahler directs should play standing up until the end (most horn players hate that suggestion) and capped by brilliant trumpets. The rest of the movement is coda: a huge Hollywood ending in which Mahler has one last surprise in store, when over a massive roll in timpani and bass drum, the entire orchestra concludes the symphony humorously with a two-note slam that's nothing more than the "sound of nature" with which it began, played hugely.

It's hard to listen to this symphony and not find that much earlier music pales just a bit in comparison. There were plenty of triumphant finales before this one, plenty of pastoral scenes, rustic dances, and even a funeral march or two. But Mahler's colors are brighter, his climaxes bigger, his tranquility calmer, his range of vision broader, and his scale more ample. In a conversation with Sibelius about the nature of the symphony,

Mahler famously remarked, "The symphony must be the world; it must embrace everything." This, then, represents Mahler's initial attempt to "embrace the world," and although it's only the beginning, you can clearly hear all of those hallmarks of his personal style that will characterize the symphonic worlds to come.

Symphony No. 2 ("Resurrection")

At the time that it was completed in 1894, Mahler's "Resurrection" Symphony (his only numbered symphony with an official title) was among the largest compositions in the history of music, and so it remains to this very day. It grew out of a symphonic poem called *Totenfeier* (Funeral Rites), composed around the time of the First Symphony, and this new piece, revised and greatly improved in terms of orchestration, became the Second Symphony's first movement.

Mahler scored the symphony for the following truly massive instrumental and vocal forces:

- four flutes (all four doubling piccolos)
- four oboes (two doubling English horns)
- three clarinets in B-flat, A, and C (third doubling bass clarinet)
- two clarinets in E-flat (second doubling fourth clarinet in B-flat)
- four bassoons (fourth doubling contrabassoon)
- ten horns (four offstage, later onstage)
- eight to ten trumpets (six onstage, four offstage)
- four trombones
- tuba
- two sets of timpani (three drums each set; maximum of three players)

- one kettledrum offstage
- crash cymbals (one pair offstage)
- suspended cymbal
- several snare drums
- two bass drums (one offstage)
- two triangles (one offstage)
- two tam-tams (high- and low-pitched)
- glockenspiel
- rute (bundle of sticks struck against the bass drum shell)
- three low bells (steel bars of deep, differentiated but non-specific pitch)
- first and second harp (several players per part)
- strings (as numerous as possible)
- organ
- soprano and alto soloists
- mixed chorus

First Movement (CD Track 2)

This first movement is a huge and stormy funeral procession, in which softer, lyrical elements constantly yield to the stern march rhythms of the cellos and basses. The conflict between these two kinds of music creates the movement's dramatic tension, and the march elements are the clear winners, although the ghostly and dark coda proves the victory to be hollow indeed.

Many of the most characteristic features of this movement, orchestrally speaking, are discussed in appendix 1 and cued to the enclosed CD, so in considering it, I would like to spend a little bit of time talking about the vexing question of originality, as it applies to the opening of this symphony and to Mahler's music in general.

The first few minutes of the Second Symphony represent a particularly interesting case, because they provide a classic example of a collision between what many commentators would regard as musically opposed (indeed irreconcilable) historical precedents: the German and Italian orchestral traditions. The opening consists of a vibrating string tremolo on violins and violas, followed by a lengthy declamatory passage of gruff statements by cellos and basses. Long passages of gruff declamation for lower strings are not new. The most famous example comes from the work that more than any other inspired the overall shape of this very symphony: Beethoven's Ninth. At the opening of Beethoven's finale, the cellos and basses engage in a conversation quite similar in tone to that at the opening of Mahler's Second Symphony.

Wagner's *Die Walküre,* the second of his "Ring" operas, also begins with a violin tremolo over stalking cellos and basses, although this "storm" motive remains a mere pattern, lacking Mahler's melodic interest. But there's another passage for lower strings so Mahlerian in tone that it's difficult to believe that it did not also serve as inspiration for this opening: the main character's entry into his wife's bedroom in Act IV of Verdi's *Otello,* just after Desdemona's famous "Ave Maria." Here, solo muted double basses (recall the First Symphony as well) embark on a long passage of melodic recitation, broken by muttering strings and quiet thuds on solo bass drum. While many commentators have picked up on the obvious Wagner connection, few bother to notice that the opening of the Second Symphony also represents Mahler at his most Verdian, and this in turn leads to a few observations that you will find useful as you travel through Mahler's musical universe.

The first conclusion that can be drawn from the above points is that the ossification of musical scholarship into national schools is really quite artificial and contrary to the reality of what most artists, be they composers or performers, actually experience as practical musicians. One of the reasons that Mahler was so disturbing to his contemporaries, and appeals to listeners now, is that he was the apostle of musical globalization at a time when narrow nationalism and (as seen today) repulsive theories of racial and ethnic purity constituted the strongest and most respectable intellectual currents of the day.

But far more importantly, the second conclusion that needs to be emphasized is this: it doesn't make any difference who does something first. All that matters is who does it best. Music history is full of composers of great originality that people couldn't care less about today, because they wrote tons of very original, boring music. Now certainly Beethoven, Wagner, and Verdi were also geniuses, so a corollary to the above observation is necessary: it doesn't matter where a composer gets his ideas as long as they are the right things in the right place and he knows what they mean and how to use them properly. Mahler knew.

The opening of Mahler's Second Symphony has Wagner's agitation, Beethoven's melodic energy, and Verdi's dramatic pacing and theatrical sense of dread. Whenever Mahler borrows, he borrows well, and like Bach, he makes whatever he borrowed so much his own that it doesn't make any difference if listeners know or care about any similarities to previous music at all. And this you will find characteristic of any great composer's work. Similarities, borrowings, and coincidences abound in our classical music tradition, but great music speaks for itself and renders the question of who borrowed what from whom an interesting but rather academic game.

Returning to the first movement of Mahler's Second Symphony, you will note that the opening writing for cellos and basses forms part of a single, vast musical idea that persists for more than five minutes. In terms of musical form, the important thing to remember is the initial brief appearance after the first cymbal crash of the lovely ascending violin theme (2:26) that Mahler develops a bit later. This anticipation of music to come constitutes an important element of Mahler's symphonic technique that recurs frequently.

This huge initial Beethovenian/Wagnerian/Verdian passage featuring cellos and basses eventually trudges to a close on basses backed by quiet stokes on the large tam-tam (4:43), ultimately leaving only the lowest notes of the two harps (5:45). You may find this repeated six-note march rhythm familiar: it occurred also in low strings (and later, low harp) at the end of the introduction in the first movement of the First Symphony.

The next passage (5:49) is an orchestral miracle and a classic instance of Mahler's use of a huge orchestra at the lowest dynamic level to create the most delicate threads of sound. Violins softly ascend as the horns begin an independent duet, only to be interrupted after a few bars by a chord on the harps. A soft call on the lower horns introduces a descending line, first on oboes, then on clarinets. The trumpets repeat the horn call, and then a new tune on solo English horn yields to the oboes and violins, with a countermelody in the bass clarinet. Next (6:53), two clarinets have yet another tune in duet, and the harp has the bass clarinet's countermelody, followed once again by the horns, violins, and finally the cellos (taking up the English horn tune). And all of this takes only about a minute! The colors are constantly changing, always in perfect instrumental balance, without ever breaking the long, seemingly endless lines of melody. This is what Mahler's scoring is all about.

As this vision of peace darkens, cellos and basses begin their steady marching once again (7:34), leading to a chaotic climax (9:50) that disperses like a sudden summer thunderstorm. Flute and harp repeat the peaceful ascending violin theme in quick tempo, and the music slowly dissolves in contentment to the quiet thuds of solo bass drum (11:15). The opening string gestures return, punctuated by tam-tam crashes and a timpani solo playing the Mahler rhythm. From the very depths of the orchestra, lower strings begin marching all over again, gradually leading to the movement's climax. Pay special attention to how Mahler approaches this climax: note the horn tune (12:48) that leads up to the general pause before the entire orchestra crashes in (with its trumpet and timpani fanfares and those mad strings whacking their bows against their instruments). You will hear this music again in the finale. After a truly crushing return to musical home base, the movement's recapitulation (15:16) proceeds more or less along the lines first heard at the opening of the symphony, save for typically varied scoring.

This time, though, the lyrical ascending theme leads to a lovely sentimental passage for strings alone (17:18), full of Mahlerian portamento and *glissando* (the strings sliding softly between notes), fading into the distance until a sinister little tremolo (18:36) takes the music from major key to minor and introduces the coda in slow march tempo. Once again, cellos and basses supported by quiet tam-tam strokes provide the background for a ghostly review of the movement's principal themes, and at the very end, trumpets colored by the swoosh of suspended cymbal hold out a tiny prospect for hope (21:23). But this time a solo trumpet denies the major key, and the entire movement collapses in a huge downward-rushing scale, followed by two soft thuds on bass drum and plucked lower strings.

Second Movement

One of the basic structural principles of the first movement was the simple contrast between quick music and slow, lyrical music. The second movement does exactly the same thing, only in reverse: the lyrical music dominates two quicker episodes. The charm and warmth of these tunes disguises the fact that they are used polyphonically: after the first episode, the opening theme returns, accompanied by a gorgeous new melody in the cellos, while the more agitated music that precedes it sounds at times like the famous contrapuntal opening of the Scherzo of Beethoven's Ninth Symphony. Though technically a slow movement, the music isn't really all that slow. It is, in fact, at least in its main sections, a graceful minuet, one of many Mahler movements written in a deliberately old-fashioned style.

Pay particular attention, after the stormy central section, to the delicious return of the principal theme on *pizzicato* (plucked) strings, decorated by flecks of harp and piccolo. The end is exquisite, the last chord deliciously timed to provide a touch of gentle humor. Note also that the music uses no percussion except timpani, no tuba, and reserves the trombones for just a few bars at the big climax (you probably won't even notice them, as they basically just enrich the accompaniment). In keeping with the music's classical-period character, Mahler gives the majority of the themes to the violins and cellos, with winds and brass providing touches of color and contrast but never assuming the leading role.

Third Movement

If the first movement was about lower strings and brass and the second movement featured the violins above all, then the woodwinds rule here. The third movement, a scherzo, is an expanded version of one of Mahler's most humorous and ironic songs, "St. Anthony of Padua's Sermon to the Fish." It's not really necessary to know what the song is about to follow the music in its watery, tipsy, slightly mocking course, and the title in any case basically says it all: St. Anthony, finding his church empty on Sunday, goes to the riverside to preach to the fish, and while he imagines that they are paying attention, they simply go about their business as they always have. It's very cute and humorous, but without words, Mahler is free to paint his emotions on a much broader canvas than that provided by the text, while preserving and indeed enriching the music's basic character at every point.

A sharp slam on the timpani sets the music going, propelled by the *boom click click* rhythm on the bass drum and *rute* (bundle of sticks slapped against the drum case), to which Mahler adds honking woodwinds. Violins offer the flowing first theme, but it's the drunken E-flat clarinet (higher and more piecing than the usual B-flat or A clarinets) that sets the tone, accompanied by strings using the wooden backs of their bows (col legno). The second time this passages comes around, the orchestra collapses in a long, tumbling run downwards, only to lead to a new theme (which you can also hear in the trio of the Scherzo of Beethoven's Violin Sonata, Op. 96). But before we accuse Mahler of plagiarism, it's worth keeping in mind that folksy melodies such as this are part of the common coin of Austrian music in general.

This section reaches a climax with pounding timpani, and over a long-held note in flute and piccolo, the strings begin what sounds like a fugue (they enter one section after the other playing the same music but starting on different notes). Suddenly a big climax capped by a cymbal crash interrupts their bustling activity, only to die away all the way down to a single flute and violin accompanied by plucked strings—a remarkable imitation of Bach or some other baroque master. The big climax intervenes once again and this time leads to a lusciously sentimental romantic tune played by a quartet of trumpets. It's moments like this that justify the presence in Mahler's symphonies of so many of the same types of instrument. The result is simply magical. Even a musical conservative such as Brahms, no great fan of Mahler the composer, loved this music, calling it "akin to genius" (which was about as nice as Brahms ever got).

This idyllic interlude dies down, and the main themes come creeping back on lower strings, but very humorously, this leads to odd harmonies that sound increasingly out of whack until the orchestra finally erupts in a derisive "Bronx cheer." The clicking rute leads the players back to the music of the very opening, which now proceeds as originally, although with distinctive changes in orchestration (note the melodic use of the drums by two timpanists). All seems to be going well as the climax that preceded the trumpet idyll returns, only to become one of the very greatest of Mahler's climaxes gone wrong. As happens in the finale of the First Symphony, the music seems to overshoot its target. To chaotic calls in the brass, all hell breaks loose, in the form of a huge scream similar to the opening of Verdi's *Otello* (Mahler called this passage a "cry of despair"). This slowly dies away as the timpani solo that began the movement returns one last time. After a few moments of reflection, the busy strings get going again, and they dismiss the whole tragic episode with the Bronx cheer.

The rute taps away as the music slowly dissolves, descending at last into a final thud from low harps and the soft swoosh of the low tam-tam (actually Mahler marks it *mezzo-forte,* or "half loud," but few conductors have the guts to play it that way). [Personal Note: I wouldn't bother to mention this last detail except to point out that the reason Mahler writes what he does is that the rest of the movements of the symphony are connected, and he clearly expects the resonance of the tam-tam to carry over to the opening of the fourth movement and for the solo voice that begins it to emerge from this percussive darkness. I have never heard what strikes me as Mahler's clear intent honored either in performance or on disc, although once when playing percussion in this symphony, I persuaded the conductor to do it this way, and the result certainly vindicated Mahler's dynamics.]

Fourth Movement

While not the first composer to use voices in a symphony, Mahler did invent the idea of incorporating whole songs into a symphonic scheme. As with all texted music, the best way to understand it is simply to follow the words as they are sung. Their meaning can be easily summarized. The singer says: "Man lies in terrible pain and need, and I would prefer to be in heaven. I happened upon a broad path, and an angel motioned me away. But I will not be rejected. I am from God and will return to God; the dear Lord will give me a little light to guide me to eternal life."

There are many remarkable features about this brief song. The words come from *Des Knaben Wunderhorn*, the collection of folk poetry that occupied Mahler for much of his early period, and the title of the poem is "Urlicht" or "Primal Light." After the alto soloist sings the opening line, the brass play a solemn chorale in imitation of church music, followed by the first stanza of the poem. This entire first section contains thirty-six bars of music (musical periods almost always fall in multiples of four, by the way), but despite the slow pacing and deliberately archaic style, Mahler contrives to give the music a remarkable feeling of "moving while standing still" by changing the time signature no less than twenty-two times! I know this sounds technical, and it is, but the point here is that because the accents never fall exactly where you expect them to, the entire passage strikes the ear as one giant melody that only comes to rest on the very last beat of bar 36.

The reason for the deceptive rhythms of the opening becomes clear when the next section begins, in which the singer describes her encounter with the angel. She is walking along a "broad path," and so the music walks with her, becoming steadily rhythmic as harp and glockenspiel mark each bar with a distinctive *ping* and the clarinet warbles a repeated seven-note figure that produces the impression of flowing movement. Two solo violins and two solo piccolos again reveal Mahler's remarkably refined use of orchestral color as the angel first appears, a moment of innocent wonder.

Anxiousness intervenes. The soloist refuses to let the angel reject her, and the mood of the opening returns as her thoughts turn to God and the promise of a place in heaven. The music dies away calmly with this message of solace, but cellos and basses rudely interrupt, the tam-tam crashes, the bass drum rolls, and the cry of despair returns more violently than ever to open the finale. And thereby hangs a particularly interesting tale about Mahler's attitude toward musical tradition and his debt to his great symphonic predecessors, Beethoven especially.

Fifth Movement

The best way to understand the relationship between the finale and what has come before is to consider the similarities between this movement and its direct inspiration, the famous choral finale of Beethoven's Ninth Symphony. Several points immediately come to mind, most obviously the use of the choir and the fact that both movements begin with a dissonant crash that returns before the entry of the voices. But the differences are equally striking. I have already noted the influence of Beethoven's "talking" cellos and basses on Mahler's first movement. What actually happens in the Ninth Symphony is that the principal theme from each of the previous movements returns, only to be rejected by the lower strings, who then hail the arrival of the "joy" theme that serves as the basis for the choral variations that follow.

Mahler does not employ the same technique of thematic recurrence from movements past, at least not in the same way, but he has understood the idea of rejection of what has come before. It's important to realize in this (and so many other) contexts that musical *ideas* are not just tunes or motives. They can be structural concepts, ways of organizing or developing musical materials, sounds of specific instruments or musical gestures, and methods for extending the music's expressive range. So Beethoven rejects themes, but Mahler rejects the specific message of the entire fourth movement. The singer offers the message of simple faith, and the orchestra responds with a huge cry of "NO!" And by saying "no" with the music of the cry of despair from the Scherzo, Mahler reminds his listeners that the answers for which the music is searching are to questions previously asked.

In other words, the first three movements offer a series of emotional states and musical images that the message of the fourth movement does not explain (at least to Mahler's satisfaction), and this gives Mahler the excuse he needs to create a complex finale on the largest scale in order to find a conclusion worthy of what has come before. Musically, the inadequacy of the fourth movement as a finale (however pretty) is achieved by the simple expedient of making it the shortest and simplest movement in the entire symphony. Think about it: if Mahler had ended there, wouldn't you leave the concert hall feeling that you'd been cheated and that the whole evening had led to a disappointing anticlimax?

So the opening of the fifth movement represents an angry reaction to the message of the fourth. However, as is usually the case with Mahler, the cry of despair with which the finale begins is not quite the same as the one heard previously. This time, the trumpets and trombones have an actual tune on top of the cry of despair, and this tune is the key to most of the music that you will hear in the half hour to come. The theme has two parts: a musical proclamation of two three-note phrases, one moving downwards, the other upwards, followed by a fanfare. As the eruption calms down, a third, ascending theme appears quietly in the horns like a vision of paradise seen from afar: this is the theme of "resurrection," the movement's eventual goal, and the first appearance of the "aspiration" or "redemption" theme that will appear in just about all of Mahler's work from here on out. This really important motive consists of a two-note drop followed by a rising scale, sometimes repeated two or three times in sequence, reaching higher each time.

The rest of the movement consists of a series of ten distinct episodes, ranging in length from about two to upwards of five minutes—a giant set of variations on this titanic opening (as well as some themes from earlier in the symphony). Each variation reveals a different stage on the journey to the symphony's transfigured ending. These episodes are very clearly demarcated by pauses or sharp changes in tempo and texture.

First episode: Offstage horns call from the distance. The orchestra responds with a brief passage (featuring oboe, trumpets, and onstage horns) that descends via mysterious trilling chords on the strings and harps to a quiet funeral march, complete with tam-tam strokes. Here is another case of a musical idea that does not require actual melodic quotation. It's impossible to hear this somber close without thinking of the first movement, and one of the ways in which Mahler greatly enriched the language of music was through his use of orchestral color as a structural tool, a way to jog your memory or bring back previous moods and images without the need to repeat specific themes.

Second episode: Woodwinds play a tune that may sound familiar: it actually comes from the climax of the first movement (CD track 2, at 12:48). Here it's accompanied by plucked strings and has a very plaintive, lonely quality. A trombone and trumpet answer the woodwinds by introducing a new tune that will become very important quite shortly, and suddenly the opening fanfare returns on the horns, only purged of all urgency and suffused with quiet light. The offstage horns then have a more melodic version of their initial horn call, leading back, once again, to the funeral march which ended the first episode.

Third episode: This is an exercise in musical anxiety, led off by a pleading English horn, shrieking clarinets, and jagged string tremolos. The musical material is all new. Clearly, this is music of doubt, and Mahler will make this obvious later on when it becomes an alto solo with words expressing exactly this sentiment.

Fourth episode: Thematically speaking, this is a very literal transformation of the second episode in entirely new scoring. Whereas the initial woodwind tune once sounded timid, now it appears solemn and confident. The full brass section plays a richly harmonized version of melody (which, you will recall, originated in the first movement), and this builds to a gigantic climax, consisting thematically of a varied return of the trumpet and trombone "answer," just as in the second episode. A drum-roll (multiple snare drums, Mahler requests) and cymbal crash introduce the horn fanfare that also came next in episode 2, and then the "answer" also returns, its phrases broken by cymbal crashes and thrilling trills on flutes and piccolo. The volume is huge, but so carefully balanced is Mahler's scoring that if you listen, you can actually hear the harps thrumming underneath it all. This leads gradually back once again to the funeral march, now at its most threatening (and ending with a killer high note for the trumpet).

Fifth episode: Two tremendous solo percussion crescendos (snare drums, tam-tams, bass drum, and timpani) separate full brass section statements of those two three-note phrases from the movement's opening. Mahler then repeats these in different positions over music of real violence that eventually becomes a full-blown parade-ground march. Strings and timpani begin with a speeded-up version of the first movement theme from the second episode, and then a fully developed marching version of the trumpet and trombone answer (from the same episode) comes back on the brass while the strings continue beneath (a technique that should be recognizable by now as typically Mahlerian). This march goes through several phases, leading to a dramatic statement of the first-movement tune in the full brass section. In fact, for a moment, the listener seems to be back in that movement—the approach to the climax is exactly the same. A pause, and with a huge crash (tam-tam, cymbals, bass drum, and three timpanists), the entire episode simply self-destructs, another climax gone wrong.

Sixth episode: The music is that of the third episode, begun on trombone and becoming a lyrical cello theme that plays against offstage percussion with added trumpet fanfares. This gathers itself up into a huge climax, which culminates in a return to the cry of despair and the very opening of the movement (as happens in Beethoven's Ninth Symphony before the voices enter). The noise stops, and we find ourselves essentially back where we started, after all of this effort. What happens next? the music seems to ask. Beethoven has the solo baritone enter immediately, with the words "Oh friends, not these sounds!" Mahler's technique is quite different, and breathtaking.

Seventh episode: Over a quiet bass drum roll, offstage horns, trumpets, and timpani engage in a dialogue, with flute and piccolo making typically Mahlerian nature sounds in the orchestra. Mysterious fanfares, drumrolls, and birdsong fill the air. Something special is about to happen, perhaps the most remarkable use ever made of extreme quietness to achieve a huge dramatic surprise.

Eighth episode: The chorus, unaccompanied, sings softly of the promise of resurrection. "Arise, yes, you will arise." The words are from Klopstock's "Resurrection Ode," as adapted and added to by Mahler himself. The music, remarkably, is a very slow, solemn version of the opening trumpet tune in its fifth-episode march variation. As the chorus sings, a solo soprano voice floats free of the vocal mass, and the orchestra answers with the "heavenly" version of the opening fanfare, as heard way back in the second episode, now combined with the resurrection theme. Mahler's scoring has never been more amazing than here, for although the music seems weightless and lit with an inner radiance, he's actually using the whole orchestra, including a full onstage brass section of ten horns, six trumpets, four trombones, and tuba! The next verse of the ode is set to the same music and leads once again to the orchestral interlude, which this time achieves a full close to quiet taps on the glockenspiel and ethereal violins.

Ninth episode: The music of the third and sixth episodes becomes an alto solo, and the reason for music's anxiety is now clear. "Oh Believe!" she sings. "You have not lived in vain. What you have striven for will be yours." She's answered in turn by the solo soprano, and then the male chorus, which sings a variation of the music of the first choral entrance. "Prepare yourself to live!" the singers shout, answered by the contralto, rising out of the mass of voices as the soprano did twice previously.

Tenth episode: The two soloists sing ecstatically of the promise of eternal life. Their song is taken up by the chorus, combining the resurrection theme with the music of their initial entrance, triumphantly accompanied by the full orchestra and organ. At their final cadence ("What you have conquered will bear you to God!"), the resurrection theme ascends into the heavens, accompanied by the pealing of bells. A final moment of quiet, like a deep sigh of contentment, leads to the final bars, in which bells, tam-tams, organ, and the full orchestra proclaim the joy of the resurrection of all mankind and of Mahler's conception of a merciful and loving creator, an idea notably free of any specific religious dogma or doctrine. Indeed, the idea of "redemption through striving" comes remarkably close to that expressed in Goethe's *Faust*, which will in turn become the subject of the finale of the Eighth Symphony and be set to some strikingly similar music.

Symphony No. 3

This symphony, completed in 1896, is the longest ever written to have earned a place in the general repertoire of orchestras the world over. It lasts around ninety-five to one hundred minutes in most performances, and it's scored for the following very large assortment of instruments:

- four flutes, all alternating on piccolos
- four oboes, one alternating on English horn
- three clarinets in B-flat, one alternating on bass clarinet in B-flat
- two clarinets in E-flat, the second doubling B-flat clarinet, the first doubled if possible
- four bassoons, one doubling contrabassoon
- eight horns
- four trumpets in F and B-flat (two additional trumpets for reinforcement if possible)
- posthorn in B-flat offstage (usually played today by a trumpet or flugelhorn)
- four trombones
- tuba
- two sets of timpani (three drums each)
- two glockenspiels
- tambourine

- tam-tam
- triangle
- suspended cymbal
- several pairs of crash cymbals (at least three)
- several snare drums (one onstage, the rest offstage)
- five to six tubular chimes (above the orchestra or in a balcony)
- bass drum
- bass drum with cymbal attached, played by a single musician
- rute (struck on the bass drum case)
- two harps
- strings (as numerous as possible)
- alto solo
- women's choir
- boys' choir (above the orchestra or in a balcony, with the bells)

Mahler divided the symphony into two parts, part 1 consisting of the first movement and part 2 taking in the remaining five movements. It's interesting but certainly not essential to know that the first movement was in fact composed last, a fact that permitted Mahler the luxury of hindsight. Knowing what was to follow allowed him design part 1 so as to cleverly anticipate certain musical features in part 2, including many of its most important themes. At the same time, this symphony clearly builds on patterns similar to ones encountered in the previous two symphonies, and these will be discovered as they arise.

Mahler also gave the various movements titles that have come down to us, although he later repudiated them. Here they are:

Part 1
1. "Pan Awakes: Summer Marches In"

Part 2

2. "What the Flowers in the Meadow Tell Me"
3. "What the Animals in the Forest Tell Me"
4. "What Mankind Tells Me"
5. "What the Angels Tell Me"
6. "What Love Tells Me"

Rather than looking at the above as a series of hard and fast definitions, it's more useful to imagine these titles as an outline, as perhaps you might have made in school before writing an essay or as I did before writing this book. The headings (which do not appear in the published score) tell where the music is going but really say nothing about how it is going to get there. For that, one has to listen, and the really important point is that it makes absolutely no difference whether one knows about these titles or not, because as in the Second Symphony, by combining movements featuring words with purely abstract sections and by constructing the piece the way Mahler does, his symphony tells even more plainly than those very words *exactly* what it is about: an evolutionary journey, beginning with the awakening of nature and life, moving up through the various kingdoms from lower to higher forms (plants, animals, man, angels), and ending with an assertion of transcendental love as the highest form of all. Quite a project, isn't it?

First Movement

The first movement is essentially a battle between two very different marches, one slow and ominous, the other lively and joyful. This is probably the most accurate description of the music that I or anyone else can offer, because in this biggest of all of Mahler's purely instrumental movements, the form is so clear-cut and the musical actors in the symphonic drama so sharply drawn that you can't possibly fail to get the point.

Eight horns in unison proudly announce the opening theme, one that has a striking rhythmic (but not melodic) resemblance to the famous "Big Tune" in the finale of Brahms's First Symphony. Actually, only the first phrase of the two tunes maintains the family resemblance (thirteen notes); after that they diverge completely, but the comparison is useful, if only to highlight the originality of Mahler's orchestral writing. Where Mahler has horns punctuated by heavy percussive thuds and capped by a crash on two pairs of cymbals, Brahms has his tune broadly sung by the traditional workhorses of the symphony orchestra, the violins. Indeed, it's probably fair to say that there are few if any German symphonies before Mahler that involve any percussion at all (beyond timpani) in their opening pages—a remarkable fact, especially when you consider that extra percussion puts in an appearance in the first few bars of Symphonies No. 3–7 and *Das Lied von der Erde* and that all of Mahler's first movements (save that of Symphony No. 10, which is a special case) take the use of the full orchestra as a given.

Pay particular attention to the second phrase of this opening theme, the one capped by the big cymbal crash. It contains three identical repetitions of a three-note rising figure, and this little motive is going to become very, very important. After the opening theme, the music settles down to a darkly wavering series of chords on the low horns (these will open the fourth movement), punctuated by soft strokes on the tam-tam and leading to a remarkably extensive bass drum solo. The point of the solo becomes clear as the steady "death rhythm" gradually emerges from the seemingly random thuds and the trombones join in, with creaky bassoon interjections between. The idea for this kind of funereal bass drum and trombone writing comes from Verdi (check out the final scene from *La Traviata*), and as with all such borrowings, Mahler heightens the color and intensity of the original, because unlike in Verdi, where this motive most often serves only as accompaniment to the voices, here it is meant to stand as an important motive in its own right. Woodwinds quickly join the procession, followed by one of the most hair-raising of all of Mahler's orchestral gestures: an upward cry on two muted trumpets. It's difficult to describe the frightening effect of this sonic panorama, the threatening upward rush of cellos and basses, thrice punctuated by stern thuds on drums and trombones, and the terrifying tremolos and trills from strings and woodwinds. Truly it's the sound of death on the march.

After the third of those terrifying thuds, preceded by upward thrusts on cellos and basses, the horns put together an actual tune that begins with the rising three-note motive thrice repeated from the opening of the symphony, accompanied by those shrill trumpet cries and what can only be called groans in the lower strings. Notice the acid color Mahler gives this tune by having half the horns play stopped tones (their hands stuffed in the bells of the instruments, making them buzz metallically) on the theme's long notes. A solo unmuted trumpet sounds a more hopeful note: this is in fact nothing less than Mahler's aspiration or redemption theme, familiar from the finale of the Second Symphony, and it will figure prominently in the fourth movement too. More shrill brass exclamations and a continuation of the horn theme lead to a rapidly descending scale on bass clarinet and bassoons that dissolves into fanfares that quickly fade away, leaving nothing but the bass drum, marching on by itself.

Suddenly, sweet chords in the flutes and piccolos, accompanied by delicate violin trills, introduce a fresh, innocent oboe theme echoed by the solo violin. If this isn't music illustrative of emerging life, then nothing can be. Clarinets interrupt with another classic Mahlerian gesture, a sort of melodic "hurrah" (six times repeated) that descends into a whirlpool of swirling strings, leading in turn to a remarkable passage for the entire percussion section at its very quietest: bass drum, bass drum with cymbals attached, suspended cymbals, triangle, tambourine, and timpani. These instruments drop out one by one, leaving nothing but the bass drum alone once again.

Bass drum and trombones begin their death march anew, and this time the Verdian accompaniment gets its aria: the longest and most impressive trombone solo ever written in a symphony (or just about anywhere else, for that matter). The inspiration may have come from the "Oraison funèbre" (Funeral Oration) second movement of Berlioz's *Grande symphonie funèbre et triomphale* (1840), but there's no hard evidence for this, and Berlioz's work is scored for a real marching band, while Mahler's is written for a symphony orchestra pretending to be a marching band, an important distinction because as with all such cases, it's the context that makes the music so surprising. Indeed, aside from that one brief solo for a single violin (and how vividly it stands out for just this reason!), those instruments contribute nothing of a melodic nature to this symphony for something like the first ten or twelve minutes, or as long as many an entire symphonic opening movement.

This fact gives you a good sense of the scale on which Mahler is working (this movement alone is about as long as Brahms's entire Third Symphony) but also explains one important reason why the progress of the music is so easy to follow: each theme has its own distinctive instrumentation. In short, the violins are coming, just not quite yet. First the solo trombone offers a dark meditation on the horn theme that occupied most of the first big death episode. At one point it seems to stop dead in its tracks, as if uncertain of how to go on. But after this moment of decision, it does indeed go on in a terrifying statement of the baleful horn theme, this time for the entire trombone section, backed by stopped horns and heavy thuds from the bass drum. This leads quickly to a fanfare, backed at its climax by triangle, cymbals, and a crash on the tam-tam, alongside repeated muted trumpet shrieks. Once again, the music dissolves in a series of deep groans from the double basses. But note this time: the bass drum has vanished, and despite its menace, that last crash evidently has had the effect of clearing the symphonic air.

The soft flute chords return along with the sweet oboe theme, but this time it's not the oboe but those agents of darkness, the double basses, that have the tune. Clearly something's afoot. Now trumpets join the cheeky clarinet hurrah, yet another indication that the players are about to change their costumes. The string section comes gushing in as before, and to quiet little hurrahs on the woodwinds, backed by a soft swoosh of suspended cymbals, a new march begins, giving the violins (but only half of them) something to do at last. Before turning to the music of this new, quick march, it's useful to compare what has been heard so far to the first movement of the Second Symphony. The music, of course, is quite different, but the concept is remarkably similar, and this offers an excellent chance to emphasize one of the more important things about Mahler and symphonic music in general: namely, that musical ideas include not just tunes, but ways of arranging them (in other words, forms.)

Both movements begin with stern funeral marches, interrupted by a contrasting glimpse of hope, or life, or good cheer, or whatever you may choose to call it. In the Second Symphony, it's the softly rising lyrical theme on the violins that's immediately snuffed out as the music of the opening returns. In the Third Symphony, it's the beginning of the quick march, also squelched as soon as it appears. Most movements in traditional sonata form keep their first and second subjects completely separate on their initial appearance, presenting them in strict sequence. Mahler's technique of foreshadowing represents a different tactic, giving the listener a taste of what is to come and then delaying the much-anticipated arrival of the second subject (and *subject* in sonata movements can mean a single tune or any number of tunes, as long as they share the same general key or tonal area) for as long as possible.

This technique creates new opportunities for the kind of dramatic surprises that most composers reserve for their development sections, and it thus energizes movements that might otherwise sound too uneventful (and formally stiff) for their length if planned along more traditional lines. It also explains why, although the form of this particular movement is perfectly clear, it's not terribly useful to discuss it in any terms other than its own or, as now, in contrast to another movement that does something similar. So to return to the comparison, even though the second subject of the first movement of the Second Symphony is a tranquil pastoral interlude (tempo from first to second subject: fast to slow), and here it's a quick march (tempo progression just the opposite: slow to fast), the organization of the material and the symphonic process is the same in both cases.

Now let's take a look at Mahler's quick march. The first thing you will notice is that after about a dozen minutes, the violins finally get the tune, at least initially. The bass drum is gone, and in its place are the light, snappy tones of the snare drum and plenty of those little woodwind hurrahs, backed by suspended cymbal. This section also contains many examples of the Mahler rhythm and generally moves with a much sharper profile than the funeral march, where all of the melodic material is based on triplets (groups of three notes played in the space of two). It's the three-against-two tension that goes a long way toward giving the opening march its creepy, slithery quality. Now, however, a good, strong, straightforward march rhythm has been established of One, two, One, two, with no questions asked, the various tunes (and there are plenty of them) all completely in sync with the accompaniment.

Finally, there is one more important participant in the family of themes and motives that make up this quick march section. After the trumpet and clarinet hurrah, cellos and violins play a little tune, beginning with the Mahler rhythm and ending with a fast version of the rising three-note motive (repeated four times instead of three) from the symphony's opening. This ending detaches itself and becomes a piccolo solo, and when it usually appears from here on out, Mahler directs that it be played accelerando, without regard for the basic tempo, and it almost sounds as though the piccolo is saying "Hurry up! Hurry up!"

So each subject in this symphony consists of a series of themes and motives, ranging in length from a single note to several minutes of music. But what knits all of the material together is that little three-note hurry-up motive, common to both march complexes, as well as to the horn tune from the very beginning of the symphony. So no matter how different in tempo, timbre, rhythm, and texture they may be, these two marches belong together like a sort of musical Yin and Yang, different sides of the same coin, sharing the same point of origin.

Hearing this music so far, it may occur to you that what Mahler has done in this movement is not so much organize a series of melodies according to conventional rules of form but rather populate a musical landscape with diverse casts of characters. And after a bit of quiet marching around in strings and woodwinds, several more of them appear. First up, on the horns, comes a new version of the symphony's opening phrase, richly harmonized rather than in unison, and it's immediately followed by the real star of the show: that sweet oboe and solo violin theme that accompanied the initial stirrings of life. Notice how it too begins with a hurry-up figure of three rising notes repeated three times. There's an organic quality to the way Mahler shuffles and recombines his phrases and motives in ever-new shapes, almost as if he's working with a form of musical DNA. The impression this gives is one of ongoing growth, which of course is exactly the point of the music. Trumpet fanfares, snare drum rolls, and timpani strokes in the Mahler rhythm accompany varied repetitions of this "life" theme, until a last series of hurrahs in diminuendo lead—finally—to the full violin section taking up the march.

The glorious passage that ensues consists of further elaborations of the life theme and eventually (on trombones) the symphony's opening horn tune, thrillingly scored for full ensemble joined by glockenspiel and tambourine. This sails grandly into what appears to be a glorious conclusion in the form of a "cadence" theme, yet another relative of the symphony's opening, capped by a truly cinematic upward thrust from the harps and strings, crowned by suspended cymbals and triangle. But as so often happens with Mahler, the triumph is short-lived. The harmony takes a turn to the dark side, trumpets blare at the top of their register, and a huge cymbal crescendo leads to a really shocking event: the return of the funeral march, more maniacally evil-sounding than ever. It's the famous Mahlerian climax gone wrong, leading the music in the exact opposite direction than you expect it to go. But even this frightening change of scene doesn't last very long. The aspiration theme returns on the solo trumpet, attempting exactly as before to break free of the funeral march's heavy grip, and with a crash on the cymbals and plenty of chaotic banging from timpani and bass drum, total confusion reigns as the entire scene dissolves into silence.

Mahler's procedure now resembles that in the finale of the First Symphony: a heroic climax that turns out to be premature and so misses its intended target, requiring the participants in that climax to regroup and start all over again. First, the solo trombone takes a musical peek around at the devastation and gives up in what sounds remarkably like trombone-style disgust. A solitary English horn then steals in with a bit of the funeral march's principal horn theme, but seems to forget how to continue as the music quietly drifts into the soft flute chords that first introduced the life theme. Bits of march music alternate with the flute chords and the hurry-up motive in piccolo and E-flat clarinet, leading to a lovely harp-accompanied duet between solo horn and solo violin, based on the cadence theme that almost brought the quick march to its triumphant conclusion. A clarinet repeats the cadence theme, under which strings and brass emit threatening two-note grunts. And now comes perhaps the most remarkable (and certainly the most demented) passage in the entire symphony.

In nonmusical terms, what happens next might be described as an attempt by a bunch of vulgar, low-class relatives of the quick-march characters to finish what the quick march itself could not. The music belongs to the same school as the klezmer/beerhall tunes in the funeral march of the First Symphony, although it's all developed from material that has already been heard, and the effect is intentionally comical— a very highly developed sense of humor being one of Mahler's most misunderstood qualities. Indeed, it's probably fair to say that from here up to the fourth movement, the music becomes increasingly humorous, and the sheer sense of fun that Mahler unleashes is very exhilarating. Cellos and basses lead off with the hurry-up theme, developing this into an extended melody that comes to rest on a series of bouncing octaves. Next, the full woodwind section, bells pointed directly at the audience, blasts out a shrill version of hurrah, only to be answered by the horns doing hurry-up in its slower, funeral-march version, backed by jingling tambourine and flatulent, oompahing trombones and tuba.

The music continues in this vein for a minute or so, hurry-up even becoming a very funny solo lick on the tuba. The hysteria quiets for a moment, and in the distance, a trumpet plays the symphony's opening theme, while the snare drum accompanies the life tune in the woodwinds. Suddenly, the opening theme blares out in the trombones as four piccolos scream the hurry-up tune in descant, just like a Sousa march. Strings gather themselves for battle as hurrah sets off a tornado of rushing scales, against which Mahler throws every march music cliché you have ever heard in your life. Hurry-up even appears as a timpani solo. As the storm runs its course, plucked double basses waddle off into the distance, and a battalion of snare drums offstage (playing in a totally different tempo) sound the retreat. If you have ever seen a war movie, you may well recognize this particular drum rhythm. Here's another one of those remarkable examples of Mahler taking something familiar and putting it to use in a startling context. There will be others in this symphony as well.

The snare drums lead to a return of the symphony's opening, but as always in Mahler, such repetitions are never quite literal. The horn theme reaches higher than before, and Mahler directs that every free hand take a pair of cymbals for the big crash (orchestras usually make do with only three sets). As the funeral march returns, the creaky little bassoon interjections are found to be missing, and the music goes straight to the trombone solo, skipping the entire presentation of the main theme on the horns. Of course, the trombone has much the same tune, so Mahler doesn't need to be so literal. Rather than leading to the big trombone climax and tam-tam crash as happened the first time around, the soloist seems to have a fit of what can only be called the blues. Cellos interrupt this nostalgic reverie, and the music of death quietly goes to sleep. The battle is clearly not going to be won by violence, Mahler seems to be saying, but rather by stealth.

Life timidly returns in a delightfully coy transition, with cellos and basses testing the waters by tossing out a few tentative march rhythms, just to see if the coast is clear, before venturing to put together an actual melody. Quiet bass drum and cymbals mark the rhythm, and hurrah joins the procession as well. From here on in it's smooth sailing, as all of the quick march tunes gradually join in and gather themselves for the final peroration. Just before the grand return of the march, played by the full orchestra, listen carefully for a tiny six-note solo on the glockenspiel, accompanied by solo trumpet. This little tag will return in the fifth movement at the words "Liebe nur Gott in alle Zeit" (love only God always). And so, with confident stride, the music cruises into its big cadence theme; strings and harps rise to the climax; and a giant crash on the tam-tam sets off a volley of brass fanfares yielding to pounding timpani (Mahler's joy motive) and, on top of it all, the trumpets blasting out the hurry-up tune. And this time, the rest of the orchestra takes that advice. With one last furious rush of strings and percussion, the quick march makes it across the finish line and closes part 1 of the symphony with a decisive bang.

Second Movement

Many performances of this symphony take an intermission after the first movement, a good idea since it's as long as your average symphony anyway. Having achieved his musical "big bang," Mahler now embarks on an exploration of the musical universe thus created, and he does it from the ground up. As with the corresponding movement in the Second Symphony, the second movement of the Third is a minuet with two quick episodes in the basic form ABABA. The brass section consists only of three trumpets and four horns, and the double basses, when they play at all, remain pizzicato throughout. The timpani get to take the movement off, and the only percussion consists of triangle, tambourine, glockenspiel, suspended cymbals, and in one remarkable episode, rute. The main themes of the movement all belong to strings and woodwinds, led off by a charming oboe solo and later by the solo violin.

You may recall these sounds from the first movement: the first stirrings of the life theme were given to oboe and solo violin, and their presence here represents a very deliberate and typical example of Mahler's achieving unity through use of instrumental color rather than literally quoting themes. The music is gracious, colorful, delicate, and highly perfumed, exactly like flowers in fact—not their physical qualities, perhaps, but rather Mahler's view of the feelings and emotions that they evoke. The A sections are full of musical dips and bows, the music very stylized, even archaic-sounding. The quicker B sections flutter anxiously like plants blown by the wind, and in the second B episode, the mood darkens considerably until, aided by fluttering rolls on the rute (a very remarkable sound, like the flapping of wings), the music gradually calms and glides gracefully to its close in the strings' highest register, with a final *ping* from harps and glockenspiel.

The movement really requires no more explanation than this. It was popular in Mahler's day as a separate piece, a fact he disliked for misrepresenting his style and, more importantly, his view of nature as both beautiful *and* terrifying. There are only two points worth keeping in mind: the first is the clear association of the main themes (purely in terms of their timbres) with the life complex of tunes in the first movement, and the second is that the music of the B episodes will return, not in this symphony, but in the finale of the Fourth. Otherwise, the music's lightness and simplicity speak for themselves.

Third Movement

This movement is, in some ways, the key to the entire evolutionary plan of the symphony, a fact that has seldom been mentioned even by Mahler specialists. The reason for this is easy to understand. There's always a tendency in a work of this size and complexity to isolate one bit at a time. You may listen to the second movement and say, "I don't hear plants, or a 'lower order' of life, of whatever." Taken alone, this will surely be the case. But if you listen to the second movement in *contrast* to the third and compare what you have heard, then Mahler's intentions become much clearer, whether you have the advantage of his programmatic outline or not, because beyond what he says, this is precisely what the music *does*.

I mentioned earlier that the two marches in the first movement weren't so much tunes as musical landscapes populated with characters. Mahler returns to this technique here. After a couple of bars of introduction on pizzicato strings, the clarinets, oboes, flutes, piccolo, trumpets, and bassoons all chime in with various birdcalls, cries, and croaks. Pay attention to the trumpet tune, a little chain of two-note sequences. It's going to matter later, and its rhythm will get a lot of exposure in different melodic shapes. The mood is humorous, cartoonish even, and each instrument has its own personalized little motive, although they all soon start tossing them back and forth among themselves. This movement has its origins in a funny little early Mahler song for voice and piano called "Ablösung im Somer"

(Relief in Summer), which describes the reaction of the forest animals to the death of the local cuckoo bird.

The simple chugging rhythms and woodwind scoring all recall in tone, if not in theme, the music of the first movement's quick march. At the first loud entrance of the full orchestra, you can hear the violins execute very graphic "heehaws," and this leads to a new passage in triplet rhythm, a roughly stamping dance on the full strings. (In terms of orchestration, this movement brings back the basses, both sets of timpani, the heavy brass, six horns instead of the previous four, and all of the percussion.) As the dance settles down, the first section returns, leading to another one of those heehaw outbreaks that culminates in a huge downward scale (something similar happened in the Scherzo of the Second Symphony), but the music continues on its contented way, taking no notice. The triplet section returns, now a bit darker in tone with quiet timpani, and very gradually, a solo posthorn (a trumpet or flugelhorn in most performances) can be heard playing in the distance.

Formally speaking, this movement has basically the same structure as the second movement: ABABA, but because it's so much longer, each section has a lot more music in it and falls readily into small subsections. So if B represents the offstage posthorn solo, this section alone would look like this: BCBDB, and it lasts a good five minutes. It is, in any case, an incredibly important solo, because it reveals where the listener is musically. The sound of the posthorn heard from afar, the way the music stops as if to listen, and the cute little C and D interludes bringing back reminders of the A section all give clues. We are indeed in the countryside, possibly in a forest, listening to a *human being* play in the distance, and all of those little motives and tunes now can mean only one thing: "critters." As if to make this even clearer, the tune played by the posthorn soon morphs into a famous popular melody: the "Jota aragonesa" used in Liszt's *Spanish Rhapsody* for piano and Glinka's *Capriccio Brillante* (Spanish Overture No. 1).

The last two times that the posthorn returns, it finds two horns playing a lovely romantic duet in counterpoint. Time seems to stand still, a moment of Mahlerian stasis, until suddenly, a muted trumpet blasts out an off-to-the-races style fanfare and the A section returns, louder and more rambunctious than ever. Note especially the very funny tuba part that grunts along with enthusiastic abandon. As the music increases in excitement, it leads once again to the big climax with the downward scale, only this time the six horns blast out a variation of the little trumpet tune from the opening, and Mahler says in his score that the playing should sound as crude as possible. Compare this music to that of the low-class invasion in the middle of the first movement: again, the tunes are different, but the atmosphere and conception are quite similar. This rises to a frantic climax as strings beat their instruments with the wooden backs of their bows while flutes and piccolos scream in distress. The posthorn solo now returns for a couple of minutes, along with its horn duet partners, and eventually comes to rest with gentle bass drum thuds. Then something quite remarkable happens.

Clarinets begin the movement all over again, repeating their opening motive over and over and the strings mount a steady crescendo. An upward glissando in the harps leads to a sound that's been heard before, although not here: it's the cry of despair from the Second Symphony, over which the trombones and horns in unison make a three-note proclamation. Unison melodies on trombones and horn are the avatars of the funeral march from the first movement. As their call rises higher and higher, a velvety stillness descends over the orchestra. Suddenly, triplet rhythms in the timpani and brass fanfares echo from within the orchestra, and with a huge crescendo, the "crude" theme rings out, first in trumpets topped with cymbals, then in trombones accompanied by the tam-tam. Under it all, the timpani pound out Mahler's motive of joy or celebration. The final bars contain a cleverly written-out accelerando, featuring strings played col legno and tambourine.

In just a few bars, Mahler has taken his listeners all the way back to the beginning of the symphony and then reminded them of how the first movement ended. The reason for this tactic is quite clear when one considers that there are still three movements to go. Mahler is saying that this third movement is indeed just a stop along the way. Progress has been made, but the danger of a relapse has not yet passed. I hope that having now heard it, you will join me in being amazed by the amount of information Mahler is able to give in this movement without resorting to words. It's a remarkable achievement in the history of symphonic music, nowhere more so than in the fact that Mahler manages it in the context of music so cuddly and adorable. You could easily imagine this movement as the soundtrack to some nature documentary about cute little wolf cubs, or koala bears, or some equally appealing denizens of the animal kingdom. No one had ever written music like this before, and no serious composer has dared do it since.

Fourth Movement

Mahler directs that the last three movements all be played together, without pause. Except for that brief outburst at the end of the third movement, it has been a long time since the music has dwelled on the symphony's funereal side, but that's all about to change. At the same time, this fourth movement runs smack up against the vexing question of what music alone can and cannot express, leading Mahler once again to clothe his ideas in song. You have seen that it isn't really necessary to know Mahler's titles to understand what is going on in the second and third movements. Indeed, you don't have to think "plants and animals" at all, because what the music embodies is not those images literally, but rather the musical qualities of, on the one hand, simplicity, charm, and prettiness, and, on the other, increased complexity through crude vigor, strong rhythms, and vivid instrumental characterization (with the posthorn thrown in to give a definite sense of locale).

But this is, in a sense, the limit to where the music can go without verbal help, and Mahler, being supremely practical about such matters, uses a text to come straight out and say unambiguously that the music is now addressing the state of mankind. This specificity, as seen in the Second Symphony, also has the advantage of confirming retroactively what has been happening in the previous movements, and it allows one to more precisely chart the music's evolutionary curve. The text comes from German philosopher Friedrich Nietzsche's *Also Sprach Zarathustra* (Thus Spoke Zarathustra), the famous "God is dead" and coming of the "superman" tract that inspired Richard Strauss to one of his most famous tone poems, the opening of which became famous as the signature music in the film *2001: A Space Odyssey*. Mahler was actually rather horrified by Nietzsche's theological position, but he found this very short "Midnight Song" just the ticket to express the human condition in the natural world (as opposed to the religious view encountered in the Second Symphony).

The music begins with those deep, low harp tones, the expressive value of which Mahler first exploited with such effectiveness. Cellos and basses play the quiet, wavering theme that immediately followed the symphony's opening horn call. "Oh man! Take heed! What does deepest midnight say?" the alto soloist intones in her best earth mother sort of voice. Against this, two horns play a gentle duet, while oboe and English horn execute a curious rising cry that Mahler asks to be played "like a sound of nature," as an upward portamento or glissando. Many wind players and conductors ignore this instruction because it makes a very strange sound, which is why Mahler asks for it in the first place. The orchestration throughout this movement is very quiet, and simply marvelous. The full requirements are: two piccolos, two flutes, two oboes, one English horn, two bassoons, four clarinets, two harps, two trombones, eight horns, and strings.

No timpani or percussion participate, no tuba, and no trumpets, but the ghost of the latter hang over the music because the climax of the movement occurs at the words "But all joy wants eternity, wants deep, deep eternity," set to the music of the aspiration theme that was first heard on the solo trumpet back in the first movement (here it also appears in the violins a few minutes before the soloist actually sings it). The words that Mahler originally set this tune to in the Second Symphony ("I shall die so that I shall live!") reveal that the aspiration being expressed is the yearning for life. This is why it appears as a more hopeful, striving element in the first movement's funeral procession, and what better expression of the human condition can there be than the desire for life and light amidst music evocative of darkness and death? Even in a symphony whose length naturally leads to the suspicion that it has a tendency to sprawl, the accuracy and economy of Mahler's perception here is pretty remarkable.

Fifth Movement

The bright sound of bells and boys' voices (placed above the orchestra or in a balcony) shatters the darkness in the most dramatic possible way. Until just before the end of the movement, the boys sing nothing but the words "bim, bam" in imitation of the bells, and Mahler specifically tells them to hold the *m* at the end and hum the note to make the effect even more realistic. Almost the entire orchestra participates with one really significant exception: there are no violins in this movement at all. (There are also no timpani.) The poem, describing the sweet singing of three little angels, is quite famous in Germany and even exists as a traditional sacred song with a melody dating back to the Reformation. As with all word settings, the text dictates the form, and the best way to listen is simply to follow the words.

The music is wonderfully scored for percussion, with bells, triangle, and glockenspiel creating a picture-postcard impression of brightness and good cheer. The entrance of the alto soloist injects a more somber note: "Why should I not cry?" she asks, to music that will be heard again in the finale of the Fourth Symphony. The angels, in the form of the women's chorus, attempt to console her, but her plea of, "Oh come and have mercy on me!" sets off a sinister little interlude, in which muted trumpets play a startling variation of the grand cadence theme from the first movement (and remember, Mahler wrote that movement last, so that theme is in reality a variation of *this* one) against the threatening *swoosh* of suspended cymbals and tam-tam. Through it all, the voices keep up their bell imitations, offering yet another example of how Mahler can turn something innocent and cheerful into music equally menacing merely by altering its harmonic and instrumental coloration.

The darkness soon passes, however, and as the women recapture the mood of the opening, the boys' chorus gets its first words, "Love only God always," set to the same music as that little glockenspiel tag that preceded the final march culmination in the first movement. You *do not* need to recognize these tiny details when listening. One can't even know for sure if Mahler was quoting deliberately or unconsciously, and the point in mentioning them serves only to emphasize the process by which he binds the movements of such a vast work together. Even if you don't say to yourself, "Aha! I've heard that before!" you will be aware, at least subconsciously, of hearing something vaguely familiar, and this is all that most composers reasonably expect.

So with the alto's threat of tears banished for good, the women and boys unite in a long diminuendo coda of "bim bam," joined by the bells, two glockenspiels, and triangle, fading into the distance until the last note, which is a final, ethereal "bim-mmmmmm." It's all over in about five glittering minutes.

Sixth Movement

The long symphonic *adagio* (very slow movement) of the type made famous in Beethoven's Ninth Symphony was, in Mahler's day, the obvious choice for expressing in music without words thoughts of the transcendental and the sublime, but even so, he wasn't taking any chances. After all, as the finale to a symphony in six movements, a slow ending was a very big risk, and indeed listeners today are apt to be disappointed by its comparative lack of variety and extravagance compared to the orchestral phantasmagoria that has preceded it. It pays to speculate a bit on the reasons that Mahler chose this particular way to end the symphony.

First let's look at the traditional association between slow music and music expressive of emotions and feelings such as love, religious solemnity, and spiritual calm. Many of these qualities are achieved simply by writing a piece of slow, quiet music in a major, "happy" key. That much is obvious. Back in the Middle Ages, musical instruments were forbidden in the performance of church services because they inevitably evoked thoughts of secular dance music and because musicians could not be relied upon to serve the needs of the liturgy without drawing attention to themselves. Instead, the preferred musical medium was unaccompanied voices moving in counterpoint or, on an even more basic level, simple chant. Both of these media have one thing in common: they are designed so as to eliminate any regular sense of rhythm and so to convey a feeling of timelessness, an impression enhanced if the tempo is very slow (though the need of the singers to breathe is a self-regulating factor in this respect).

It's fair to say that all musical instruments have one of two purposes: to create rhythm or to sing as voices do. The rhythm section belongs to the percussion, particularly to those instruments that do not make definite notes. The most vocal instruments are those that rely, as the human voice does, on breathing. Woodwinds and brass can often come very close to imitating the inflections of the singing voice, and the way that they phrase a melody will necessarily be quite similar, even when the tune they are playing is not tied to a text. In fact, some composers of the Renaissance and Reformation periods would actually put the words of religious music under the instrumental parts (by this time the players had made it into church), expecting them to be played with the same attention to phrasing and the same religious devotion as if they were being sung.

That leaves the strings. They can hold notes indefinitely, execute acts of fantastic agility, slide around between notes with great precision, and in short, do all sorts of things that voices can't. But the real issue is sustaining power, a quality they share with the one wind instrument accorded a regular place in religious observance: the pipe organ. This makes them perfect for both slow congregational singing in sustained chords and seamlessly spun contrapuntal lines that seem to go on forever. When played thus (*legato,* or "bound together"), strings are also the least clearly rhythmic of instruments, able to move from one note to the next with no perceptible accent or attack. So they make the perfect vehicles for expressing qualities of solemn spirituality. In other words, the less vocally oriented the music, the more spacey it sounds.

So taking the above points for granted, there are only two ways to achieve this timeless, transcendental quality in instrumental music. One way is to have no melody at all and simply write comparatively rhythmless textures consisting of shifting timbres and note patterns. Many modern composers do just this, but the often scary or alien-sounding results are not usually what is associated with the concept of spiritual love. "Neptune," the last movement of Gustav Holst's *The Planets,* adopts this method. The other way is to write very slow music, with a clear melody, rich contrapuntal texture, and just enough rhythm to make it sound like a song too big and grand, too cosmic, for mere human beings to sing, but nevertheless one which listeners can understand and feel moved by. This is what Beethoven first did in his Ninth Symphony, and it's Mahler's technique here. There are very few adagios of this sort in the symphonic literature; Mahler wrote four in total.

There is a world of contrast between the fifth and sixth movements. The fifth movement purports to be about angels and a happy assertion of faith. But the music says something else entirely. The rhythmic ringing of bells summoning worshippers to church, the snappy rhythms, the simple folksy melodies—clearly this music is about religion, but not necessarily about spirituality. There aren't even any violins! This is, in short, a good-natured parody of the conventionally religious viewpoint, religious kitsch if you will, similar in its way to the fourth movement of the Second Symphony. And Mahler has arranged things so that his listeners find it no more satisfying a culmination or endpoint for this symphony than it was for the previous one, however charming the music (and necessary the contrast with the movements that precede and follow). He wants to go beyond the expression of specific doctrine and instead offer a taste of the real thing, the next step up on the symphony's evolutionary ladder. Fortunately, here he's on very firm ground, because just as music cannot self-evidently express the idea of the human condition without words, it has no need of them at all to suggest feelings of transcendence, mystical awe, spiritual peace (or divine love, or whatever you choose to call it).

It should come as no surprise, then, that Mahler begins his finale with (for the first time in the symphony) an extended passage lasting several minutes, given only to the string instruments. In a movement that can last anywhere from twenty-one to twenty-eight minutes in performance, time seems suspended as the music floats quietly forward. And look at the extensive directions Mahler gives the players: "slowly," "calm," "with feeling," "very legato," "very expressively sung," and all this before the first note has even been played. But this being Mahler and contrast being the lifeblood of his method, there's a snake in this particular garden, and victory is not granted without struggle. It must still be won. We have arrived at a wondrous place and now must prove ourselves worthy of staying there.

And so, after that long, calm, opening paragraph, a new, "sad" strain begins, introduced by only a few desks of strings and leading to the first entrance of the woodwind instruments, in this case a solo oboe singing a broad lament. The music quickly gains in passion and rises to a climax, marked by the horns playing a five-note unison motive that is more than just reminiscent of the storm scene at the opening of Verdi's *Otello*. A conscious borrowing? Who knows? What matters is that it is the right thing in the right place here. As the music regains its composure, cellos and violas lead gradually back to the opening theme on the violins, now decorated with an equally solemn counterpoint in the woodwinds.

The sad interlude returns on horns, with solo violins gently commenting, and the oboe tune gains intensity as transferred to the violins, rising quickly to a moment of passion and just as quickly returning to the sad music (on woodwinds this time). Once again the strings develop the oboe lament, the music gaining strength and rising at last to a tremendous climax, at the apex of which the horns blast out hurry-up, just as they did when introducing the principal theme of the first movement's funeral march. This shocking intrusion stops the music dead in its tracks for a moment, before it resumes its calm progress with a more flowing version of the opening theme—and in this connection, note that the opening theme is a several-minute-long river of music composed of a variety of phrases that Mahler rearranges as suits his purpose. Right now, his purpose is to reach an even bigger climax based on the "good" tunes rather than the sad ones, but this leads to an even more surprising intrusion: the return of the quick march's big climax in the version that went wrong halfway through the first movement. The *Otello* motive in the horns also appears, adding to the nightmare, and with a series of crushing timpani rolls, the music skids to another halt.

I mentioned above that a firm rhythm is the enemy of the transcendental, because that makes music sound like either a march or a dance of some kind, either one of which is about as unspiritual as you can get. So when Mahler uses timpani in this movement (until the very end), they play nothing but rolls. The only other percussion instruments he permits are bass drum, also used only for a couple of rolls, and two cymbal crashes. One has just been heard, and there's one more to come.

So the music has once again stopped dead. A flute and then a piccolo grope upwards in a couple of lonely, broken phrases over mysterious string tremolos, and then yet another recollection of the first movement is heard: that moment of decision in the middle of the trombone solo. What will happen next? Will darkness return? You already know the answer from my previous comments, but that doesn't lessen the surprise Mahler has in store, because not only is his answer a return to the calm music of the opening, but it's played as softly as possible by the least likely of all instruments given what has been heard so far: the brass, trumpets and trombones in particular. Pity the players: after an hour and a half of blowing their lips off, this is a hellishly difficult passage to get through, requiring enormous control and sensitivity, and it's a rare live performance that manages it flawlessly. But when it happens, it's glorious.

Now the music pushes confidently onward, achieving the triumphant climax (and the second cymbal crash) that eluded it three times before. The brass intones the movement's opening bars with maximum force, and the theme slowly seems to recede into the distance, reaching at last a calm plateau of tremolo strings. Trombones and trumpets begin the opening melody again, and at that moment you may notice its family resemblance to the very horn call that began the symphony, but just as this possibility becomes clear, a huge crescendo intervenes, and the timpani boom in with a tremendously sloweddown version of Mahler's joy motive. It is, in fact, the ending of the first and third movements that Mahler brings back to complete his symphonic journey. The slow tempo and broad, confident strides give the celebration the necessary larger-than-life transcendental quality at the same time as they round off this unprecedentedly huge work in musically satisfying fashion.

Symphony No. 4

Despite the mystique that surrounds so much of the creative process (and classical music in particular), I have to confess that I find the stories behind the writing of most pieces of music to be for the most part uninteresting, often amounting to little more than a sort of "What did you do at the office today?" litany for musicians. Certainly such tales reveal little of the mystery of genius and of the creative process that leads to masterpieces. Mahler, who was also a full-time conductor, only had a few weeks during the summer to devote to composition, so in his case, the story behind the writing of his symphonies is actually closer to the answer to that old grammar school essay favorite: "What did you do on your summer vacation?" The Fourth Symphony, though, really does have a fascinating history, because it bears directly on the experience of listening, particularly if you come to it chronologically, having just experienced the Third Symphony.

Back in 1892, Mahler composed a song based on a text from *The Youth's Magic Horn,* his favorite collection of folk poetry and the source for so much of his vocal music. He called the song "The Heavenly Life," although the original title is "Many Fiddles Hang in Heaven," and he thought of it as the mirror opposite to another song, "The Earthly Life," which recounts the story of a starving child who passes away before the season's grain can be harvested, milled into flour, and baked into bread. The two poems really do complement each other, as the central image of "The Heavenly Life" concerns all manner of food available free for the taking and in general describes the total absence of want and worldly care.

Mahler clearly loved this song. It became one of the very few recordings of him in performance that exists (at the keyboard in the form of a piano roll). In fact, he loved it so much that he decided that he would use it as the finale of the Third Symphony, and as this song preceded all of the other movements in that work, he was able to design the symphony so that its second and fifth movements actually quote themes from "The Heavenly Life," and there are other, more subtle, binding elements as well. Perhaps the most interesting of these, mentioned in the previous chapter, is the fact that the first, third, and sixth movements of the Third Symphony all have an ending featuring Mahler's joy or celebration motive of pounding timpani. No doubt, had the symphony contained a seventh movement as originally planned, the ending of its adagio sixth movement as it exists now have it would have been considerably different, because "The Heavenly Life" ends with this motive too, transformed into a gently rocking lullaby on the low strings of the harp.

At some point, however, for whatever combination of musical and expressive reasons, Mahler decided that this cheerful, simple song would have made for a terribly disappointing anticlimax to the world's longest symphony, particularly after the epic adagio that constitutes the current finale, and so he decided to save this movement and use it instead as the finale to an entirely new symphony, the Fourth, making it the first symphony ever to end with a song, and also giving him the chance once again to design the remaining movements so as to lead inevitably to the finale. What he came up with is a humorous, sunny, and mellifluous work that he thought would become immediately popular.

Contemporary audiences and critics in fact hated it with a virulence that truly shocked him, although in retrospect, perhaps it shouldn't have. Coming after the huge preceding works, it seemed to them like a cheap musical joke. They were correct—after a fashion. What Mahler in fact wrote was an anti-romantic symphony, one which pokes fun at the stylistic clichés of the day, not the least of which is that a symphony must be a big, heroic work with an especially impressive, grand finale. Much of the music is very funny, the finale most of all, but as so often with Mahler, the music operates on several levels at once, and behind the symphony's delight in childlike innocence and simplicity, there's also a healthy dose of practical wisdom.

The scoring is remarkable for what it does *not* include:

- four flutes (two doubling piccolos)
- three oboes (one doubling English horn)
- three clarinets in B-flat, A, and C (one doubling E-flat clarinet, another doubling bass clarinet)
- three bassoons (one doubling contrabassoon)
- four horns
- three trumpets
- one harp
- timpani
- suspended cymbals
- crash cymbals
- bass drum
- triangle
- glockenspiel
- sleigh bells
- tam-tam

- strings
- soprano solo

Note the absence of trombones and tuba. This is the first clear evidence of Mahler's intention to cut the traditional romantic symphony down to size. Not even the archconservative Brahms omitted the trombones from his orchestra, and despite the typically lavish deployment of winds and percussion, the absence here of heavy brass signals not just a very different approach from Mahler's previous symphonies, but the dawn of a new way of thinking about orchestration and also the first glimpse of the neoclassical aesthetic that dominated the music of the decades immediately following Mahler's death. In this, as in so many other things, he pointed the way forward for succeeding generations.

First Movement

The symphony opens with the gentle sound of sleigh bells decorating little "chirps" in the flutes. The first thing to keep in mind here is that although this particular percussion instrument is usually called *sleigh bells* (since this is the picturesque association its sound brings to mind), Mahler said that it represented the bells on the court jester's or fool's cap, which is a very different matter: one that clearly signals his comic intentions. This sound of flutes and bells also constitutes perhaps the most vivid and instantly recognizable musical gesture that Mahler ever created. It colors the entire symphony, providing for instant recognition based on the use of percussion tone color alone. So when the jester's bells (as I will call them) return in the finale along with their accompanying woodwinds, it's clear that Mahler has found a fresh yet incredibly simple method of organically linking the movements of the symphony together, one that does not rely on the time-consuming process of repeating whole themes.

This entire movement is, in fact, one of Mahler's cleverest, a sort of anti-sonata that pretends to observe all of the rules while simultaneously making fun of them. It starts, after the jingling introduction, with a gentle tune on the violins evocative of Haydn and Mozart. Classical practice dictates that the exposition section of a movement in sonata form contains melodies capable of development later on. This usually means that they break up into different figures, or motives, that can be recombined into different shapes, and so Mahler has designed his first theme with this in mind, but with a vengeance. It's classical-style music on steroids. Each phrase has its own rhythmic shape and special orchestration, and all of these figures are going to get shuffled around and recombined in the most amusing ways later on. The best way, therefore, to understand this movement is to pay special attention to these opening themes.

After the first phrase on the violins, cellos and basses answer with a rising scale in what's called *dotted rhythm* (after the way it's notated). This means, in practice, an expanded version of the Mahler rhythm: "dum, dadum" simply becomes "dum, dadum, dadum, dadum...etc." Remember this rhythm. It practically defines the tunes of the finale. The next motive is a little horn sequence consisting of a melodic turn followed by three repeated notes. Keep in mind those three repeated notes; you won't believe what's going to happen to them. Violins then turn the scale in dotted rhythm upside down, oboes and clarinets get the horn motive, and then the whole series repeats itself (listen to the clarinet and bassoon motive behind the violin's first phrase) with a slightly different and expanded initial answer from cellos and basses, leading in crescendo to a fresh and very childlike clarinet theme that ends in the strings rushing downwards. This entire concatenation of phrases, rhythms, and motives constitutes the first subject of Mahler's anti-sonata.

The second subject begins in the cellos with a tune in popular song form: that is, four phrases having the shape AABA, the climax being the more fully scored return of the A phrase. If you listen carefully, though, you will notice two things about A: it contains the motive of three repeated notes very prominently, and its last five notes are the same as the last five notes of the symphony's initial violin phrase. In short, although it sounds new, the second subject actually builds on elements from the first subject—a tried and true classical-period strategy, because it will allow interesting combinations and transformations of themes as they develop later on. Mahler even provides a closing or cadence theme to bring the exposition to its conclusion. It begins on oboes and bassoons alternating with strings, and it also features three repeated notes, as well as the downward-rushing scales from the end of the first subject. Its effect is very comical if the conductor observes Mahler's indicated "breath pauses" and abrupt shifts in tempo and dynamics.

As this dies away to the gruff tones of a solo double bass, the jester's bells and flutes return, as if to signal the classical-period habit of repeating the exposition entirely. Indeed the first subject comes back, but rather than literally repeating it, Mahler varies the shape of its phrases, and instead of leading to the second subject, the music veers off in another direction entirely, like a car taking a wrong exit off the highway, and slides gracefully into a pretty episode based on the tiny clarinet and bassoon motive that made a brief appearance under the initial return of the first subject's first phrase in the violins. You may not have noticed it, so discretely does Mahler sneak it in, but if you go back and listen, you'll find it with no trouble at all. This diversion has a delightful effect: it upsets the movement's goal-oriented sonata form by suggesting that the music has nowhere in particular that it needs to go and can take its own sweet time in getting there.

The jester's bells return yet again, and by this time, the movement seems not to really be in first-movement sonata form at all but rather following the pattern of many classical finales in behaving like a *rondo,* which is simply an expanded verse-and-refrain song form in which a repeated A section alternates with episodes of differing character. A typical rondo might take the shape ABACA, or something along those lines. A solo violin begins this new episode with the rising scale in dotted rhythm, leading to the horn/wind motive from the first subject and then the violin's opening phrase. What is heard is actually the entire opening theme, but in the phrase order 2–3–1 instead of 1–2–3. This seeming confusion throws the music off into yet another digression, a delicious episode in which four flutes in unison over pizzicato double basses—and further accompanied by that clarinet and bassoon motive from the last episode—put the motive of three repeated notes together with the dotted rhythm of the strings' rising and falling scales.

Just as it's now absolutely clear that the movement really must be a lighthearted rondo, Mahler begins a huge passage of what is clearly development. For the next couple of minutes, all of the motives that have been heard so far enter into a whispering, conspiratorial conversation as they get tossed from one group of instruments to the next. The three-repeated-note figure becomes especially important, as a sneer on muted trumpets, a perky commentary on winds backed by suspended cymbals, a dry snapping of strings struck with the wood of the bows, and finally (in dialogue with the opening theme), a triumphant fanfare on solo trumpet backed by timpani and repeated strokes on the tam-tam (which most performances never allow to register cleanly). As the excitement builds, the glockenspiel plays the clarinets' childlike theme, while the entry of the bass drum signals impending disaster. The passage culminates in a crash on the tam-tam and the trumpet fanfare turning into a scream of frustration, yet another of those characteristic Mahlerian climaxes gone wrong.

But now something delightful happens, because nothing in this symphony goes wrong for long. As the trumpet keeps muttering away at a tune that will ultimately become its opening solo launching the Fifth Symphony, the jester's bells return along with bits of the violins' opening theme, all jumbled up and confused with the initial flute chirps and roulades, until the music essentially says "Oh, the hell with it!" and simply stops dead. After a moment of silence for the orchestra to regain its composure, the violins gently enter with their rising scale in dotted rhythm, and we're back at the beginning as if nothing unusual or frightening had happened at all. The effect of picking up the conversation in the middle is very funny, and it plays right into Mahler's anti-sonata plan by telling us that the effect of all of that complicated development stuff was precisely—nothing.

And so the music approaches the climax gone wrong from a slightly different direction, this time with jubilant cymbals and timpani, and this time all goes well and the orchestra lands squarely (with a satisfying *thump* in the drums) at the second subject, now more richly scored and broadly sung than ever before. This leads once again to the jolly little woodwind cadence theme and so to the return of the jester's bells, yet again signaling the entry of the violin's first subject, once again in different phrase order and now leading back to that relaxing, initial diversionary episode on the cellos based on the innocuous clarinet and bassoon motive. This may sound complicated to read on the page, but you'll recognize it instantly when you hear it.

This motive rises slowly through the string section, becoming softer, higher, and calmer, until a solo horn signals "time to wake up." The strings respond lazily with a few plucked chords.

Violins barely have the energy to whisper the first phrase of their opening theme, but as the cellos and basses sneak in with their rising scale in dotted rhythm, life and energy return, the horns belt out the motive of three repeated notes, and the movement comes to a cheerful close on two crashing chords.

The structural humor in this movement doesn't really require that you know what sonata form is; merely that you catch the tension between music that wants to relax and music that wants to do something dramatic and either gets diverted or winds up in a mess whenever it tries. This is the concept that defines Mahler's anti-sonata, and the movement certainly speaks for itself in this respect. However, there's no question that the more familiar you are with the music of Haydn and Mozart, the funnier at least some of Mahler's jokes will sound, and the deeper and richer your perception of his sense of humor will be. This does not strike me as being particularly disadvantageous. There are, after all, many poorer ways to spend your time than in getting to know some Haydn and Mozart.

Second Movement

Mahler made the ghastly mistake of letting slip a few verbal remarks about what this movement represents, and as usual in these cases (as he himself feared), the minute talking begins, listening stops. He called the movement "Friend Death Tunes Up!" (that's actually a sort of loose English translation of the German original, but you get the picture). And so the idea that the deliberately mistuned solo violin represents a sort of child-ish German bogeyman has remained attached to this music ever since. It may well do just that as far as Mahler was concerned (assuming reports of what he said are both correct and com-plete), but it surely doesn't demand that other listeners accept the same view, especially those who may have no idea of who "Friend Death" is in German children's literature.

I have never given much thought to what the bogeyman might sound like in a symphonic context, and even if I did, I doubt that he would sound like an incorrectly tuned violin. Nor does the fact that this is the only official word that has come down to us mean that Mahler believed it to be the most important thing about the music. For example, no one ever seems to mention that the solo horn has just as big a role in the movement as does the solo violin, possibly because Mahler never indicated verbally what the horn represents—Friend Death's brother-in-law, perhaps? Mahler would, in any case, never have been foolish enough to limit his options and write a movement that depends on anyone possessing such knowledge.

The second movement is a scherzo in ABABA form, although as always with Mahler, the repetitions are subtly varied and rescored on each recurrence. More than anything else, this is nature music, with an outdoors flavor. Mahler tells the solo violinist to play "like a fiddle" with a rough, scratchy tone (tuning the strings a tone higher than usual helps), and as noted above, a good deal of the "solo" music isn't really solo at all, but a duet with the orchestra's principal horn (anticipating the hugely important horn solo in the Scherzo of the Fifth Symphony). But aside from these two solo turns, the music is full of nature imagery: bird calls, watery sounds, buzzing and chirping winds, all in a graceful *Ländler* (waltz) rhythm. The very opening, a solo horn call followed by a birdlike cry in the oboes and bassoon, sets the music's expressive parameters, and only then, to a spidery accompaniment of strings and clarinets, does the solo violin enter with its whining principal theme. This little horn and woodwind introduction also serves as a transition between the movement's various sections and, in fact, has the last word.

The A section itself has an interesting form, sort of a mini-rondo with the violin solo constituting the refrain (or *ritornello*), and it can be described in letters as abaca. The *b* episode is a cute little tune for oboes with a high kick at the end of each phrase (based on the opening horn call), followed by a jolly answer on the clarinet. The second episode (that is, *c*) is a watery stream of notes in the violins with little screams at the end of each phrase, the musical equivalent of letting out a surprised yelp after being pinched on the behind. Note here, as in the first movement and indeed throughout the symphony, Mahler's very sensitive use of percussion at low volume. Within this opening section, timpani, bass drum, suspended cymbals, triangle, and glockenspiel all contribute to the proceedings, but always discretely, little dabs of color shading the orchestral canvas.

The movement's introduction returns, and then the solo horn assists in the transition to the first trio section. (The word *trio* is simply conventional terminology used to describe any contrasting episode in a dance movement, like a scherzo or minuet, and has nothing whatsoever to do with the number three.) This is a slower stream of melody, initially on clarinets, like a burbling brook. Every so often, those same clarinets pretend to be trumpets and shout out a strident little fanfare featuring the Mahler rhythm before sinking back into the general air of contentment. The mood gradually darkens and then the introduction takes the listener back to the Scherzo, greatly enriched in orchestration, its solo violin now in duet with the solo horn. The music proceeds in the same order as previously until the expected arrival of the trio section, this time introduced by solo trumpet.

This trio section features the same tunes as before but with two surprises. First, a normally tuned solo violin comes in towards the end, revealing a tender side of the soloist's personality. Second, just as listeners expect the return of the A section, the harp ushers in a luscious oasis of luminous beauty, complete with violin glissandos sliding between notes and trumpeting clarinets. It's one of those marvelous moments in Mahler that walks the borderline between sentimentality and kitsch. So lovely is it, in fact, that the Scherzo never quite gets its bearings on its final return. The dance becomes hesitant and threadbare, the orchestration more sparse and chamberlike. Timpani bring back the music of the introduction, darkened by gentle strokes on the tam-tam and quiet bass drum thuds. The softly threatening mood continues until hiccupping cellos lead to a final bird call—a sly wink from four flutes, three oboes, two clarinets, triangle, glockenspiel, and harp that dispels the darkness with a final *ping*.

Third Movement

This big Adagio (usually around twenty-three minutes long in performance, plus or minus a couple of minutes), like all of the movements in this symphony, expresses the tension between tranquility and drama, blissful calm and anguished agitation, but it does so in a much more serious vein than has been experienced previously (although it has its humorous passages too). In terms of structure, it's basically a set of alternating variations on two contrasting themes, one in a major, happy key and the other a minor key lament. The movement accordingly falls into four big sections of roughly equal length, followed by an explosion leading to a transfigured coda. But Mahler adds a twist by having both themes accompanied by the same rhythmic figure, a five-note idea in plucked lower strings, harp, and (later) bassoon, like the quiet tolling of bells. Various commentators have agreed in calling this five-note figure a "bell motive," and I will too.

The movement begins, like the adagio finale of the Third Symphony, in a state of transfigured calm, with a long passage for the strings in a hypnotically slow tempo, the bell motive tolling beneath. Oboe, bassoons, and horns add their voices in gentle chorus as this first strain comes to a close. Mahler marks the second theme "much slower," but the tempo actually seems to increase, because both the bell motive and the lament (played by the oboe) are written in much shorter note-values. After the initial oboe phrase, violins enter with the most important gesture in the entire movement: Mahler's aspiration or redemption theme, a series of phrases that rise upward and fall back, rise higher and fall back again, reach higher still, and finally collapse with a huge downward groan on the horns. This entire complex repeats itself with even more passion (at one point in its life it was used as a perfume commercial, which says something about its overtly emotional character, I suppose) and finally dies away to the speeded-up version of the bell motive on solo violin and harp.

Now the tempo increases, and a flowing variation of the opening returns, again scored mostly for strings (the cellos lead), with gentle counterpoints in the winds. It glides along without a care in the world, finally expiring as its stream of melody surprisingly finds the strings imitating the downward groan that ended the previous section. Like a premonition of tragedy, this signals the winds to reintroduce the lament in a beautifully desolate passage scored only for oboe, English horn, and French horn playing delicately intertwined contrapuntal lines. The violins enter with the aspiration theme, and once again this rises to two huge climaxes, ending by exactly the same process as did the previous section: that is, by anticipating what is to come—in this case, another variation of the opening theme. You can follow these variations quite clearly because they feature our old friend from the first movement, the motive of three repeated notes.

Now comes the movement's fun part. Mahler treats his listeners to four variations, each faster than the one that has come before, and one leading to the other with sudden lurches to the new tempo. This process comprises the "variation version" of what happened in the first movement: increasing speed and complexity leads to complete confusion. It culminates in a zany and cartoonish race to the finish line spurred on by solo glockenspiel (a most unlikely visitor to a solemn adagio such as this, as you may recall from the discussion of the finale of the Third Symphony). A crash on the cymbals and a solemn gesture by the horns herald a return to the mood of the opening, calmer than ever, and the music slowly dies away to the deep sounds of the bell motive.

The movement could end here, and sounds like it has every intention of doing so, but Mahler has one more card up his sleeve. You may recall that all of the previous movements managed to shrug off or explain away their dark sides. This one hasn't yet, but it's about to do it in the most dramatic way imaginable: through divine intervention. Strings give a great cry, and the entire orchestra explodes with what sounds like a single brilliant chord. In reality, the entire string section is actually playing a series of fast arpeggios—the notes of the chord in sequence—so that the whole texture sounds energized. Trumpets blast out the Mahler rhythm in long notes, the harp goes crazy with glissandos, cymbals crash, and the bass drum thuds (in that order), timpani pound out the bell motive with both sticks bashing each drum, and behind it all, the horns play the opening theme of the finale.

This loudest, most violent climax of the entire symphony has a remarkable result. It introduces the aspiration theme, but in a form closer to that heard when it first appeared in Mahler's music, as the resurrection theme in the finale of the Second Symphony. Gently confident now, purged of all angst and passion, it calmly takes the orchestra by the hand and leads it to the gates of paradise, specifically one of the most heavenly key changes in all of music. The slow violin glissando in octaves that completes the transformation will either bring tears to your eyes or have an effect similar to fingernails scraping on a blackboard, depending on how well-tuned it is in performance. The music becomes all top and bottom, high violins, flutes, and clarinets against deep tones in the harp and basses (still playing the aspiration theme in long notes). It strikingly resembles the "space music" of Holst's *The Planets,* written some fifteen years later—especially "Venus, Bringer of Peace." And that's exactly how the movement closes, in perfect peace, ideally setting up the finale.

Fourth Movement

Now comes the movement around which Mahler composed the entire symphony, a song for soprano and orchestra. In fact, Mahler planned the piece for boy soprano, and the score simply marks the part "singer" with no further specifics in this regard, but tradition uses a light professional woman's voice, which guarantees the symphony more frequent (and, one presumes, more accurate) performance. In recent times, certain conductors (Leonard Bernstein for one) have revived the use of boy soprano with mixed success, and it remains a viable option, justified, in the event, by the final results. Modern day countertenors (high-voiced male singers who take the roles formerly reserved for castratos in baroque opera) also take the part from time to time. No matter who sings, the artist in question must absolutely obey Mahler's instruction: "The voice with a sincere, childlike expression, always without parody!"

The reason for this instruction is twofold: the words are themselves grotesque and only make sense if delivered perfectly straight, and the parody elements are present in the orchestra in the interludes between verses. These bring back the jester's bells from the first movement, but whereas in that context (played quietly and gently) they represented innocent joking, here, played loudly and obnoxiously, they represent the intrusion of the worldly and mundane, an unwelcome reminder of what the Adagio supposedly left behind.

What exactly is Mahler up to here? This movement has been described as "a child's vision of heaven," which it most certainly is not. The words make it clear that it concerns, rather, a heavenly life, in which "Saint Peter in heaven looks on." In his Second Symphony, Mahler asserted his belief in an afterlife. In the Third, he moves beyond the religious clichés of that work's fifth movement to attain a more basic, spiritual reality, arising from nature and the evolution of ever-higher forms of life and consciousness. But now that he has arrived at heaven, what is Mahler to do? The artistic challenges of depicting any sort of paradise, let alone an afterlife of eternal bliss, in terms other than those of dullness, have vexed everyone who has tried, from Dante on forward. Mahler's solution is to say: "All we can do is dream of what it would be like to be children once again, without a care in the world." That's as close as one can get in terms we can understand here on this earth. It's a remarkably shrewd answer.

So the singer describes childlike joys: dancing and singing, all kinds of food available for the asking; the local butcher Herod provides meat from animals that willingly offer themselves for human consumption, and the angels bake bread (I told you it was grotesque). The singer's opening tune takes over those skipping, dotted rhythms from the first movement—and even more of the thematic material has already appeared in the second and fifth movements of the Third Symphony as well. There are four verses separated by jester's bell interludes (which, incidentally, also feature the motive of three repeated notes), and the best way to understand the music is simply to follow the words as they are sung.

As the third jangling refrain dies away, a wonderful calm settles over the last verse. When the singer describes the incomparable music provided by St. Cecilia and her assistants, the melody takes off on a brief flight of the special Jewish/Slavic music that Mahler so often saves for these moments of intense nostalgia. But Mahler reserves his subtlest touch for the very end. As the soprano sings "The angel's voices gladden our senses, so that everything awakes to joy," it becomes clear that the music is doing just the opposite—it is, in fact, going to sleep. The entire final verse is a lullaby, suggesting that everything heard previously exists only in our dreams of childhood. And so, to the gentle tolling of the harp (the joy motive that closed the first, third, and sixth movements of the Third Symphony), the symphony quietly subsides and vanishes out of hearing. It's almost impossible to hear the actual moment where the last low note of the double basses finally stops.

It's worth taking a moment to see how writing a work around this particular finale has led Mahler to turn his back on yet another tradition, that of the romantic symphony with the grand finale, a tradition to which his first three symphonies, in their various ways, all pay homage. Mahler was, by nature, a romantic artist, who plainly loved symphonic drama on the most heroic scale, and who also found himself quite attracted to the romantic notion of the artist as hero. But like his colleague Richard Strauss, he was very ambivalent about this idea as well.

Approaching the same issues within the German symphonic tradition, Mahler freed himself from the usual "tragedy to triumph" expressive curve established in such works as Beethoven's Fifth and Brahms' First. In the Fourth Symphony, he realized that there were some ideas that music could express only by approaching them from a different direction than that most often dictated by the contemporary school in which he was working, particularly the one that required that a grand finale resolve the issues raised in the long and complex first movement. From here on, all of Mahler's symphonies contain elements that may very well be considered classical or anti-romantic.

What this means practically is that Mahler's symphonic structures—the number of movements, their architecture, and their sequence within each new work—may or may not be traditional in a textbook sense, but he often strikingly recalls the great Viennese classical masters (Haydn, Mozart, and Beethoven) in that a new intellectual brilliance and formal ingenuity balances and disciplines the music's extravagant emotional expression. This is bad news for diehard, self-styled romantics, who believe that emotional spontaneity cannot coexist side by side with a learned, even scientific, approach to composition, and unfortunately this prejudice (for that is what it is) is still very much with us. Essentially anti-intellectual more than it is pro-romantic, this common view has long downplayed the critically important (and musically wonderful) classical side of Mahler's artistic personality. Here, on the other hand, it will be celebrated for the astonishing flowering of genius that it represents.

Symphony No. 5

The scoring of each of Mahler's symphonies often says something very interesting about what one can expect from the music itself. The Fifth Symphony has the fewest number of woodwinds in relation to the brass than any other comparable work in the series, leading to the logical assumption that Mahler has something special in mind for the brass and string sections—an assumption that in the event proves to be entirely correct. The symphony requires the following orchestral forces:

- four flutes (all doubling piccolo)
- three clarinets in B-flat, A, and C (third clarinet doubling clarinet in D and bass clarinet in B-flat and A)
- three oboes (third doubling English horn)
- three bassoons (third doubling contrabassoon)
- six horns
- four trumpets in F and B-flat
- three trombones
- one tuba
- timpani (four drums)
- bass drum
- a second bass drum with cymbal attached, played by one musician

- crash cymbals
- suspended cymbals
- triangle
- glockenspiel
- tam-tam
- snare drum
- slapstick
- harp
- strings

Mahler completed his Fifth Symphony in 1902, but he revised it completely shortly before his death in 1911. It is his first symphony since the First Symphony that does not require vocal forces, and far from making its message more abstract or ambiguous, its lack of verbal specificity actually makes the music easier to understand simply as music. The previous three symphonies, which combined movements having a sung text with those for orchestra alone, necessarily force discussion in the direction of explaining the way in which the various parts with words relate to the parts without them. Here, on the other hand, Mahler has the option of being as specific or as vague with his musical imagery as he likes and of leaving the interpretation of what it all means up to each listener.

Mahler needed words, not just because he wanted to express ideas that required them, but also because by using them, he was able to explore new and unusual musical structures that would have lacked purpose and inevitability without the justification of a text. This was a real problem for romantic composers working in the German symphonic tradition, where the formal rules were often at odds with both artists' expressive aims and their clear knowledge (via Wagner and other great nineteenth-century opera and theater composers) of what the modern orchestra could do. Indeed, this was so much of a problem that Mahler removed an entire movement from his First Symphony to turn it into a four-movement symphony as compared to its original designation as a five-movement symphonic poem.

The Fourth Symphony showed Mahler how to get past the problem of the romantic "finale symphony," the pressure that post-Beethoven composers often felt to create works with triumphant grand finales, despite the fact that conventional classical form tends to put the greatest formal weight and complexity in sonata form first movements and dictates that finales should be more simply organized, lighthearted rondos. No composer approached this problem more practically, successfully, or ingeniously than did Mahler. After writing three symphonies with three very different types of triumphant finale (both vocal and purely instrumental), he produced the anti-romantic Fourth Symphony, in which the weightiest part is neither its first movement nor its finale, but rather its third-movement adagio.

The Fifth Symphony carries this formal experimentation even further, placing greatest emphasis on the huge central Scherzo, possibly the only symphony in history ever to adopt a structure of this type. Flanking the Scherzo are two pairs of movements. In each pair, the slow initial movement serves both as an introduction and source of thematic material for the longer, more complex one that follows. Mahler then connects both pairs by having the big brass chorale that erupts at the end of the second movement return as the climax of the symphony's finale. It's a wonderfully imaginative and unique symphonic structure.

The Fifth remains the toughest of all Mahler's symphonies to bring off successfully in performance, not because it's uniquely long or complicated, but because of how hard it is to play, especially for the strings. It probably has more fast music in it (counting the Scherzo) as a percentage of the whole work than any other symphony of Mahler's, and because it's not a full evening's length (it usually runs about sixty-five to seventy minutes, or about as long as Beethoven's Ninth), it generally appears on the second half of a standard concert program—meaning that most orchestras and conductors will have a hard time sustaining the necessary energy until the very end. Mahler always insisted that his music come first on any program so that the orchestra would be fresh, and indeed at one of the first performances of the Fifth, the players had to follow up this most tiring of symphonies with Richard Strauss's every bit as taxing *Sinfonia Domestica!* The brass players must have felt their lips about to fall off, and Strauss was quite annoyed that Mahler had left the band completely exhausted.

Practical performance problems aside, however, few symphonies are as expressively clear as this one. The negative, hostile, or sad emotions are mostly concentrated in the opening two movements, which Mahler designated part 1. Peace, tranquility, happiness, and humor reign in the last two, called part 3. The Scherzo, part 2, serves as a giant fulcrum, partaking of both worlds while effecting a transition between them. This is, in fact, really all of the explanation you will ever need to understand the emotional curve of the music, but of course the details are so interesting that they repay closer consideration.

Part I

First Movement

The symphony opens with a cliffhanger: a difficult solo for trumpet that must be played perfectly, because if it isn't, it has an incredibly demoralizing effect on the entire orchestra. The trumpet's tune actually has a long and illustrious history, being a true Austrian military signal. It appears as the prelude to battle in the second movement of Haydn's "Military" Symphony, and it's well known to pianists as Mendelssohn's *Song Without Words*, Op. 62, No. 3 (also a funeral march). Mahler presents it in the most shocking possible light: the orchestra enters on two glorious major chords and it seems as if the tune foretells victory, but the harmony darkens, and with the entry of the snare drum and the tune now hammered out by the full ensemble, it sinks into darkness, with a falling horn call in the Mahler rhythm repeated three times.

This is now familiar Mahlerian funeral march territory, with rhythmic death figures on the trombones (derived from Verdi's operas) and quiet bass drum thuds and tam-tam strokes. Cellos and violins enter with a long, sad melody full of tiny hesitations, wavering between heartbreak and consolation (that is, between minor and major keys). This leads back to the opening, rescored so as increase the music's feeling of desperation and despair. The cellos and violins return, and now Mahler extends their melody and adds the accompaniment of tam-tam, muted snare drum, and the marching band combo of bass drum and cymbals struck by one player, all at the lowest dynamic level.

As the string threnody comes to a gentle close in a somewhat hopeful major key, with the quiet *swoosh* of suspended cymbals, the trumpet mutters its opening theme, and suddenly all hell breaks loose. Wild strings backed by off-beat "Italian opera" rhythms in the trombones support a wailing song of despair on solo trumpet (the trumpet truly leads this movement, just as the solo horn will characterize the Scherzo). At the height of the music's fury, the opening trumpet call returns, punctuated by timpani solos and leading back (via a very effective roll on the bass drum) to the initial hysterical outburst. Note the rising theme in the strings that cuts across this new trumpet solo: it will feature very prominently in the second movement.

The orchestra rushes to a huge climax, and as the horns grope upwards, the entire episode self-destructs over bass drum and suspended cymbal rolls, topped by one of those Mahlerian trumpet screams.

The opening military call returns yet again, heralding the most brilliantly scored climax so far (and some very difficult high notes for the trumpets), but this is no more effective than it was previously, and the music sinks back into darkness exactly as at the beginning. The cello and violin threnody returns, only this time scored entirely for the wind and percussion sections, with a single viola and solo trumpet adding nostalgic counterpoints. The strings soon reenter with their message of consolation, and the threnody quietly marches to a close. Solo timpani play the opening trumpet call, and the violins begin a new lament to a quietly chattering accompaniment. This joins the rising phrase from the end of the previous outburst, and the music gains intensity as the violins increasingly recall that turbulent music. Trombones pick up the rising phrase, and with a wrenching scream, the entire orchestra crashes in with a long, slow decrescendo of despair, capped by rolling snare drum and suspended cymbals.

Once again the opening trumpet call returns, leading to a dark brass chorale underpinned by quiet strokes on the tam-tam. As the gloom deepens, the trumpet continues muttering its opening four notes, and you may stop to consider that these four notes strongly recall those of another, even more famous Fifth Symphony—Beethoven's. (The significance of this will become clear shortly.) One last time the trumpet call returns, now accompanied by nothing more than the dry clacking of strings played with the wooden backs of their bows. A solo flute at last takes up the trumpet's lonely challenge as the bass drum quietly rolls between the tune's broken phrases. And with a single pizzicato thud from violas, cellos, and basses, the move-ment comes to an inconclusive end.

Second Movement

The opening funeral march was a slow movement with quicker outbursts. This second movement is its mirror image, a quick movement with slow interludes. It opens "stormily agitated, with the greatest vehemence," the music recalling in mood if not in theme the funeral march's hysterical first episode. Listen first to the little three-note woodwind shrieks just before the first cymbal crash (a few seconds into the movement). These formed part of the chattering accompaniment to the funeral march's second episode, and they will become positively ubiq-uitous very shortly. Pay particular attention also to the string of descending four- and five-note figures that comprise the violins' first theme (right at the first cymbal crash). They will detach themselves—usually with the top note held longest—and become an important factor, not just in this movement, but in the entire symphony.

For a brief time, over a heaving accompaniment in the lower strings, the violins put together a broad tune, but constant interruptions from the brass and rhythmic instability quickly tear it apart. Like virtually all of the climaxes in these first two movements, this one soon self-destructs to the sound of those descending five-note figures in strings, then brass (just before the cymbal crash that blows it all to bits). I've noted before that one of Mahler's characteristic fingerprints is the climax gone wrong—one that leads somewhere you didn't expect or has a surprising outcome. He also takes great advantage of the "climax that leads nowhere at all." The music basically runs into a brick wall and just stops. It gives a very effective impression of frustrated, unresolved rage. This entire huge paragraph of orchestral upheaval constitutes the first subject of a movement basically in classical sonata form, but as with most of Mahler's mature examples, you don't need to know anything about this when listening. Just take it as it comes.

The second subject should sound familiar. It's simply a rescored version of the funeral march's second episode, and recognizing it shouldn't be a problem, since it was heard just a few minutes previously. The chattering accompaniment now belongs to the winds rather than the strings, and you'll notice that the chattering actually consists of two combined elements: a series of rapidly repeated chords and the little three-note woodwind squeals heard at the beginning of the movement. What makes this little accompanying motive so marvelous is that its elements can appear together or separately and the repeated chords vary in length from three notes on up. This gives the music both textural interest and a curious, almost "blurry" quality, since neither the tune nor its accompaniment ever sounds quite the same, even though they are instantly recognizable whenever they return.

There's one more aspect of this tiny figure of just a few notes that makes it so interesting and further provokes what we might call a memory reaction in most listeners. When the motive has three repeated notes ending on a longer one, it actually becomes the rhythm of the famous "fate gesture" in the first movement of Beethoven's Fifth—as well as recalling the symphony's opening trumpet call. Of course, Beethoven's theme is a stern knocking at the door, while Mahler's is an ironic chuckle mixed with a whine. So I don't want to push the resemblance too far. It is worth noting, though, that creating a feeling of musical unity in this fashion, by transferring simple rhythmic motives from one movement or thematic group to the next, is standard classical procedure. Mahler learned it from Beethoven, and so this subtle homage from one master of symphonic writing to his great predecessor is both touching and entirely appropriate.

The second-episode tune that the cellos spin out over this chattering accompaniment opens with three repetitions of the Mahler rhythm, a pattern we have also heard before in the falling motive after each climactic appearance of the trumpet call in the funeral march. The cello theme is soon joined by its companion, the rising figure that led (on the trombones) to the funeral march's final collapse. Here, however, it actually takes over in the form of a lovely extension to the initial melody, and in this form, it will dominate the remainder of the movement.

This tune comes around twice, the rising figure achieving real warmth as played by the strings, although the quiet strokes on the tam-tam signal a warning. Sure enough, the music of the opening returns, leading quickly to a leaping climax based on the Mahler rhythm and a quick disintegration as the brass play the descending five-note scale, just as previously. The music mutters to a stop, with only a drumroll linking this passage to the quiet cello recitation that follows. This incredibly lonely music actually grows out of the three-note woodwind cries that we heard at the movement's beginning and as part of the chattering accompaniment to the second subject. It calmly works its way back to the full second subject, this time played by low horns. Once again the tam-tam signals a warning, and the Mahler rhythm in its descending form, as heard in the first movement, returns on muted horns, trombones, and trumpets.

A flurry of activity in the lower strings causes the orchestra to rush forward, until suddenly, a sequence of three-note cries in the violins brings us back to the middle of the first movement funeral march. The effect here is similar to what happens in the first movement of the Fourth Symphony after its central climax gone wrong: it seems as if this music has been going on all along behind the scenes, completely unaware of the preceding turmoil. The funeral march gradually morphs back into the second subject, and with another lurch, the woodwinds announce a new tune full of false cheer. How do you know it's false? Well, you have to hear it for yourself, but it has something to do with the awkward rhythms and thumping timpani. This tune leads to what attempts to be a triumphant climax, complete with timpani pounding out Mahler's joy motive, but it shouldn't be too surprising when this too goes wrong and a tremendous crash on the cymbals launches the recapitulation.

Three-note cries on the strings, punctuated by bass drum thuds and maniacal laughter in the trumpets (in the form of a really sinister descending scale), and with another crash we're back at the beginning, even more violently than before. When we come to the roiling accompaniment in lower strings, Mahler surprises us by taking a musical shortcut and bringing the second subject back directly in the violins. Its second half, initiated by the rising figure (now in the horns), sounds more purposeful than ever and ultimately leads to yet another cymbal crash, which for one terrifying moment brings back the funeral march's hysterical first episode, complete with wailing strings and solo trumpet. The rising figure intervenes immediately attempting to restore order, but the brass persist in repeating their descending motives of four and five notes, and with a sense of total despair the trombones bellow the descending five-note scale (backed by the tam-tam) like wounded animals. Beneath them, the second subject on the strings gropes upwards, only to entangle itself in the same descending five-note motive.

Now comes a remarkable passage of confusion, in which the strings play a series of three-note cries, the horns have the descending motive (four notes instead of five this time), timpani thud in the background, and the whole passage gives the remarkable impression of trying to escape from a sort of musical blind alley by running in circles. Salvation duly arrives: the three-note cry in the brass turns into a blazing chorale in which the entire section blasts out fanfares against rushing strings and swirling harp. Mahler has in fact calculated this passage so carefully that he puts the word *climax* into the score, complete with arrows pointing to the exact note that marks the culmination of all of this brassy perorating.

As this climax dies away trailing clouds of strings and horns, the woodwinds slither back in with sinister whirring scales. A few three-note cries, and with a sudden crash/thud from cymbals and bass drum, the music of the opening returns for the last time, permeated with four- and five-note descending scale motives. With a terrific crash on the tam-tam (Mahler marks it *triple forte* and writes "let it reverberate") and one especially panic-stricken five-note phrase in the brass, the music disintegrates completely. A muted trumpet sounds an epitaph, and gently pulsating strings introduce the ghostly coda: the basses play fragments of themes (including the by now ubiquitous descending motive that, as you will see, in fact returns to conclude each part of the symphony). Flecks of triangle and harp produce tiny sparks of color and the muted brass offer one last glimpse of the chattering figure, while the three-note cry filters down from solo viola to solo tuba. Timpani alone have the last note ("Correct tuning!!" Mahler writes, knowing timpanists only too well).

So ends part 1.

Part 2

Third Movement (CD Track 3)

Welcome to the largest scherzo in symphonic history. At nearly sixteen to eighteen minutes in most performances, no other movement of its kind in the general repertoire equals it, either in length or in importance within its parent work. Mahler knew that he was on to something special when he wrote this scherzo, even to the point where he expressed the desire to conduct it fifty years after his own death, just to show everyone how it ought to be done and, in particular, to make sure that it wasn't played too quickly.

He had good reason for concern: there's a lot happening here, and the music needs to take its time, both to make the best impression and also to establish itself as the symphony's center of gravity. A meaningful minute-by-minute description in words isn't really possible, because in the time it takes to describe what you are hearing and why it matters, the music will have long since moved on, and as the themes themselves represent Mahler at his most entertaining and ingratiating, the mere act of listening virtually guarantees enjoyment and comprehension. On the other hand, I *would* like to spend some time talking about how this movement functions within the context of the symphony as a whole because this accounts in large part for its very special character.

In my initial comments about the Fifth Symphony, I said that the Scherzo acts as a transition between parts 1 and 3, sharing elements of both. I want to be very clear about what this means, because you don't write a sixteen-to-eighteen-minute-long movement in waltz tempo that lives entirely on the scraps of other movements. All of the music here is in fact original; none of it borrows from the first two movements or contributes themes to the last two, with the one significant exception of the descending four-or-five-note motive that figured so prominently in the last movement. However, as these chapters on the individual symphonies have been at pains to make clear, there are many ways besides obvious thematic borrowing to unify a large symphonic structure and provide a feeling of organic relationship between the various parts. Musical ideas come in many forms. Think for example of the Third Symphony, where the first movement's trombone solo has an analogue in the third movement's offstage posthorn, the idea here simply being that of having important themes delivered as extensive solos for brass instruments.

In the Fifth Symphony, one sees exactly the same idea put to similar use. The first movement is dominated by the solo trumpet, almost to the point where parts of it could be an actual concerto for that instrument. The Scherzo features another big brass solo of concertolike proportions, this time for horn. Of course the music is completely different, but the idea of a big movement led by a solo brass instrument is the same. Similarly, the finale features lots of busy contrapuntal string writing in a quick tempo, while part 1 has little or none at all. The Scherzo, though, is full of exactly the same kind of texture that initially occurs when the solo horn is not playing, and it's in thematic contrast to it. These string passages belong, in character if not in actual theme, to the world of part 3. There's also a contrasting slow waltz for strings featuring the Mahler rhythm, which gets "infected" by the horns as the music proceeds, gaining in energy along the way. So one might say that the brass section dominates part 1, the strings rule part 3, and the two sections share the Scherzo equally, with woodwinds and percussion as neutral parties throughout.

Mahler reinforces the musical archetypes at work by also making a very strong rhythmic contrast between the horn's solo passages, which swing along in waltz tempo, and the episodes characterized by the regular, chugging string counterpoint that effectively negates the feeling of being "in three" (and of dancing altogether). This contrast means that the two kinds of music are different enough in their basic elements that Mahler doesn't have to restrict himself when it comes to imaginative uses of instrumental color from section to section. There's plenty of lively string writing in the solo horn episodes, and plenty of brass mingling with the contrapuntal sections (and woodwind solos accompanying everybody), but I'll bet that if you think about these episodes after you've heard them and try to remember what they sounded like, you will remember "horn" about the former, and "busy, chugging violins" regarding the latter, no matter what else may be happening at the same time.

Here, then, is a brief overview of how Mahler presents the movement's principal thematic material in the first few minutes, cued to the accompanying CD:

1. Horn music in waltz tempo (a), leading to
2. Chugging strings below a rhythmic four-note figure for three clarinets in staggered entrances (b) (0:43)
3. Both *a* and *b* repeated and varied (for example, the clarinet rhythm shifts to the trumpets at 1:30)
4. Slow waltz, mostly for strings (2:22)
5. Horn music interrupts suddenly, *a* returns (3:17), and with a loud push from the timpani (3:44)
6. *b* gets expanded into a big contrapuntal episode for strings with the descending five-note motive from the second movement on top in muted trumpet (4:06)
7. A sudden hush (4:27) leads to a mysterious quiet melody on horns backed by woodwinds with more of the descending motive on trumpet

8. The movement's opening horn gesture leads to a big climax
   (5:00), featuring a bass drum roll over tremolo strings and
   huge blasts from the horn section

This is a lot of material for Mahler to play with, and while
the movement as a whole broadly follows the traditional ABA
pattern of most symphonic scherzos (what I've just described
constitutes A), in reality, the calm middle section (B, or trio),
merely develops material already heard. The return of A continues this development, with new scoring and increased energy
and brilliance. So as the Scherzo proceeds, you will hear these
two worlds—brass and strings—intermingle, and it is this
cross-fertilization of timbre and texture that constitutes the
real business of the piece, linking the symphony's first two
movements with its last two by combining the two characteristic kinds of music that typify parts 1 and 3 in the same way
that they will ultimately come together at the very end of the
symphony.

The way Mahler accomplishes this gradual metamorphosis is
easy to hear if you simply pay attention to what the horns and
strings do as the movement proceeds. For example, the lead-in
to the quiet trio section features a soft string chorale alternating with horn calls (5:19). At its heart (7:04), the violins
and solo horn sing a duet in softly lyrical counterpoint. As the
music accelerates wildly towards the recapitulation (9:25), horn
cries alternate with furious passages of scurrying strings (introduced by loud timpani thuds). When at last the opening returns
(10:04), after a ferocious battle (9:43) between the horns and
the four-note clarinet rhythm (hammered out by trumpets and
slapstick), Mahler begins to mix together all of the tunes that we
have heard so far, in particular giving the slow waltz (originally
for just strings) to the brass section at the original quick tempo
(11:18). This leads ultimately to a huge, primal-sounding climax

(13:33) that strips the music of melody altogether and consists instead of pure timbre: the blasting of horns superimposed on the texture of frantic string counterpoint. It's almost as though some process of musical fusion has unleashed an explosion of elemental horn and string energy.

These two contrasting forces, plaintive horns and chugging strings, separate again temporarily for the long transition to the coda. This begins (15:21) with a bass drum solo rapping out the clarinet/slapstick rhythm, but Mahler has a big surprise in store: all of the main themes return, played simultaneously on top of one another, in the raucous closing bars. Note especially the descending five-note figures repeated over and over in the trumpets (15:56), which, as previously heard, figured prominently (if quietly) at the end of the second movement. The very same idea (in its four-note version, also played by the trumpets) will wrap up the finale too.

So when, at the very end of the symphony, Mahler brings back the brass chorale from the second movement in combination with the theme of the finale's string fugato (a *fugato* is basically a passage written in counterpoint where all the parts are based on the same tune), listeners hear something familiar, not just in terms of the melodies involved and the instruments that play them, but in the very act of combining them. Thanks to the Scherzo, this procedure has also been well established and reinforced through repetition over time. It resides in listeners' subconscious memories, adding to their sense of satisfaction at the symphony's close. In this way, Mahler ensures that the conclusion of part 3 truly represents the end of the whole symphony, and not just the last twenty-five minutes or so.

The primary importance of the Scherzo of the Fifth Symphony, then, lies in the fact that it actually describes the method by which Mahler intends to unite the two disparate worlds of the symphony's outer parts. This is why the movement is so long and must never be rushed. Mahler wants his listeners to hear this process at work through the myriad examples the movement gives—to let it sink in to memory gradually—and along the way, to entertain as much as possible, so that the entire operation simply becomes a function of enjoying the range of moods that the music expresses: happiness, fun, nostalgia, bravura, and perhaps a touch of loneliness here and there. Play the music too quickly, let it pass by in a blur, and this sense, not just of what the movement *is*, but of what it *does*, will be lost.

You may or may not recognize at first encounter the Mahlerian logic at work in using the Scherzo to prepare for what happens in the finale, but you will surely feel the sense of rightness and inevitability that comes from the underlying formal symmetry and balance that Mahler achieves in presenting his material this way. This is, in fact, Mahler the classical composer in action, creating unique symphonic structures in response to his expressive needs, and in doing so, energizing the tension between the music's disciplined intellectual brilliance and its always uninhibited emotionalism.

Part 3

Fourth Movement

This adagietto, for strings and harp, was for many years the most famous single movement in all of Mahler, not least due to its use in the film *Death in Venice,* but also because it inhabits a special world of romantic tenderness. Its form couldn't be simpler: ABA, although as usual with Mahler, the return of A isn't literal, but subtly varied. The string writing is what might be described as warmly diaphanous, like one of those deliberately blurred photos of a beautiful woman whose soft edges only emphasize the subject's sensuous curves. The contrast with the opening of part 1—the trumpet solo—confirms what the Scherzo has already told us, namely, that this symphony's emotional journey from despair to happiness is going to be articulated in terms of the instrumental opposition of brass and strings.

But the most important aspect of this movement isn't its A sections, lovely as they are, but the central episode, which consists of an old friend: Mahler's aspiration theme. This motive consists of a two-note drop, followed by a rising phrase, leading to another drop, and repeating this pattern several times. In fact, the end of this section repeats the exact same pattern heard after the big climax in the Fourth Symphony's Adagio, the upward-rising scales reaching towards a transfiguring change of key. Remember this tune; something quite marvelous is going to happen to it later on.

There's a big controversy in Mahler scholarship surrounding this movement, the argument basically running that it is now played too slowly. It is known that in Mahler's day some performances lasted around eight minutes, while today ten to twelve minutes isn't unusual, and some conductors have stretched it out to as long as fifteen minutes. I take no position on this issue: it depends on the quality of the string playing, the conductor's overall conception of the work, and the conductor's ability to sustain whatever tempo he or she selects. The world of classical music is full of claims of exaggerated importance made on behalf of minor interpretive issues, and this is certainly one of those.

The return of A leads to a dreamy coda that somehow manages to rise to a sonorous climax, followed by a very long dying fall, but the movement doesn't actually come to a full close. The strings hold onto the last chord until it's interrupted by—you guessed it…

Fifth Movement

...the horns!

Mahler calls this movement a rondo, which in the classical period generally means a quick movement having the form ABACA, etc. Rondos can be shorter or longer, and the non-A sections, or episodes, can contain anything, but the principal determinant of the form is the fact that the main theme, or ritornello, does just what the word implies: it keeps returning. It goes without saying that Mahler has his own special take on this particular formal structure, because not only does he want it to do everything that a rondo is supposed to do, he also wants to: (1) mirror the form of part 1, in which the second movement borrowed themes from the slower first movement; (2) demonstrate in retrospect that part 3 also has something in common with part 2 (the Scherzo) and so represents the second half of the tale that the Scherzo tells; and (3) tie up the entire symphony by making this movement the culminating point, not just of part 3, but of the entire work.

You already probably have a pretty good idea of how some of this is going to be accomplished. In fact, I've already discussed how the symphony ends, but there's much hilarity along the way, so let's see how Mahler organizes this breezy and surprising finale, which has the basic form: introduction – rondo: ABACADAE – coda.

Introduction

Horn and woodwinds unfold a series of perky little tunes, some of which come from an amusing Mahler song called "In Praise of a Lofty Intellect." The song tells the story of a singing contest between a nightingale and a cuckoo, judged by a donkey. You can probably figure out who wins. This alone tells something about what to expect in the movement to come, but the most important thing to notice is that this introduction contains another well-known character: the descending four-or-five-note phrase (here in the four-note version from the second movement). This phrase leads to the:

Rondo

A. Ritornello
This sunny melody, sung by horns and accompanied by strings, culminates in a little celebratory fanfare in the woodwinds and then plunges right into the:

B. First episode
Now comes that busy, contrapuntal string writing first heard in the Scherzo. The strings enter section by section, and over this activity, various cheerful motives from the introduction appear in varied procession, including the descending four-note phrase. A couple of interruptions in the form of flatulent blasts from the brass produce some floundering by the strings, while the winds recall bits of the introduction, taking us back to the:

A. Ritornello
This returns more or less as it was just heard, only now played by the strings with support from the horns (in other words, with the instrumental layout of melody and accompaniment now reversed). This glides effortlessly into the:

C. Second episode
This starts with the same bustling string writing under horn tunes from the introduction, just as in the first episode, but before it can be defined as more of the same, it eases into a graceful, speeded-up version of the aspiration theme from the

middle of the Adagietto. Here, then, is the part 3 analogue to the sharing of melodic material that happened in part 1. This charming interlude winds down and the string counterpoint returns, leading to a breezy climax that skids into the:

A. Ritornello

Actually, this is not an exact repetition, but a variation mostly for the strings that comes to resemble the original ritornello increasingly as it proceeds. Don't worry if you don't catch the resemblance immediately. Its whole purpose is to provide a vigorous rhythmic contrast that gets upset by more of those amusingly flatulent interruptions from the brass, this time underpinned by timpani, sending the music briefly back to the introduction and, in particular, its descending four-note motive. These interruptions create even more commotion than before, which quickly sorts itself out in the form of the:

D. Third episode

Basically, this is a slightly varied repetition of the second epi-sode, complete with the aspiration-theme interlude and an even bigger climax that reintroduces the:

A. Ritornello

Another variation, this is scored almost exclusively for strings in rich, robust counterpoint (five independent parts). The tune is very close to that of the original ritornello and follows its shape very faithfully. After a sudden pause, the music jumps back into the:

E. Fourth episode

The four-note descending phrase takes over the trombones atop contrapuntal strings, and this causes the most amusing moment yet of general confusion (all the brass join in). A final rush of string counterpoint now rapidly builds to a huge climax, with thunderous rolls on timpani and bass drum until the brass section slams on the brakes in the most graphic possible manner, and with a sudden change of key and diminuendo, the music leaps into the:

Coda

This begins with those descending four-note phrases calmly repeated in all kinds of ways, accompanied by chuckling woodwinds. The strings bring back the aspiration theme, at which event the woodwinds execute little celebratory hurrahs. As the sonority builds, the brass sound a fanfare, the strings fling themselves into the main theme of their contrapuntal episodes, and the great chorale from the end of the second movement returns, more resplendently scored than ever. It rises to a huge climax, capped by cymbals and bass drum, and the four-note descending phrase in the trumpets signals the race to the finish, in which violins, brass, timpani, and cymbals create a whirlwind of sound. The violins break free, only to be slammed to a halt by one last belch from the brass. Woodwinds unleash a stream of laughter, and after a last four-note descending phrase in the horns, cymbals and bass drum slam the symphony to a close.

So here you have it, exactly as advertised, a finale that justifies everything that has come before but that doesn't require a text or any other sort of verbal explanation to do it. It uses themes from the Adagietto, just as the second movement took from the opening funeral march. It makes as much play with the descending four-or-five note phrase as did the second movement and Scherzo, ending part 3 (and thus the entire work) in a manner similar to parts 1 and 2. It makes the Scherzo's contrapuntal string textures the engine of its forward progress, and it culminates in a return of the brass chorale from the second movement, combined with the main string theme of the various episodes. And it accomplishes all of this in a mood of good-humored ribaldry, those brass interruptions graphically coarse.

Mahler's Fifth Symphony lacks the transcendental qualities of the previous symphonies. It does not aspire to grand philosophical statements about the human condition. Rather, it undertakes to say: "I can write a symphony that begins in the depths of black despair, with a funeral march, and ends in a mood of pure slapstick, and I can explain it every step of the way through the purely symphonic logic of organizing my themes, motives, and movements accordingly." It's undoubtedly fair to say that no work of purely orchestral music before this one had ever attempted to cover such a vast emotional distance from beginning to end, and few since have done so as successfully.

Symphony No. 6 ("Tragic")

Mahler composed his "Tragic" Symphony between 1903 and 1905, but as with all of his works, he continued to adjust and tinker with it practically until his death in 1911. He scored the piece for a fabulously large and varied assortment of instruments—indeed, the biggest orchestra he ever used in a purely orchestral context and one of the largest ensembles ever brought together by anyone. Here it is:

- piccolo
- four flutes (third and fourth also doubling on piccolo)
- four oboes (third and fourth also doubling on English horn)
- English horn
- clarinet in E-flat and D (alternating with fourth clarinet in A)
- three clarinets in B-flat and A
- bass clarinet in B-flat and A
- four bassoons
- contrabassoon
- eight horns
- six trumpets in B-flat and F
- three trombones
- bass trombone
- tuba
- timpani (two players)

- glockenspiel
- xylophone
- crash cymbals (several pairs)
- suspended cymbals
- bass drum
- two snare drums
- deep bells
- rute (bundle of sticks rapped against the bass drum case)
- tam-tam
- deep tam-tam
- small wooden stick (tapped against the bass drum case)
- hammer
- triangles (several)
- cowbells
- four harps
- celesta (two or more if possible)
- strings

This is the full orchestration: even the list of instruments in the critical edition doesn't account for everything, especially regarding the harps and percussion, and very few performances actually go to the trouble and expense of supplying Mahler's complete compliment of players when it comes to the doubling parts. On recordings, where balances can be adjusted by microphone placement, this matters less than it does in live performances, although one can certainly sympathize with cost-conscious orchestra managers faced with extravagant demands for extra harps or several celestas (especially when Mahler writes for the difficult-to-find German model with its extra-low notes).

There has been more nonsense written about this symphony than any other work by Mahler, a fact indicative of both its unique character and the difficulty most people, even academics, conductors, and other supposed experts, have in dealing with a piece of pure instrumental music as powerful as this one. Most of the problems originated with Mahler himself, at least as reported by his none-too-reliable wife Alma in her book on him, and arise from the conflict between his programmatic intentions and what he ultimately wrote. There's no real mystery here, but because what Mahler reportedly *said* about the piece is known (at least to a limited extent, at an early point in the symphony's genesis), this has all but obliterated people's ability to simply listen and take note of what he *did*. So here is a comparison of what Mahler allegedly claimed about it and what the music that he actually wrote expresses.

A "Tragic" Symphony

Here's one incontrovertible fact: Mahler did indeed call the Sixth his "Tragic" symphony, although the published score gives no indication of this and he did not designate the work by any official title. Contemporary reviews also confirm this appellation, including one marvelous cartoon in which Mahler stands next to a huge collection of percussion instruments and exclaims, "My God, I've forgotten the motor horn! Now I'll have to write another symphony!" But what, in this context, does *tragic* mean? Let's be very clear on one critical point: the word does not necessarily mean "death," despite the fact that most tragedies end unhappily and this symphony is Mahler's only one that does not embrace either a triumphant or peaceful major key conclusion.

In order to understand what Mahler means when he says the music is tragic, it's useful to recall the definition of the term as the ancient Greeks conceived it: a *tragedy* in a staged drama reveals the impotence of man's heroic striving against an uncaring, implacable fate. By evoking the emotions of pity and terror for the sufferings of a heroic protagonist of noble character, tragedy creates in the audience a feeling of *catharsis,* a purging of negative emotion produced by the sympathetic identification of the viewer with the titanic struggles of the characters on stage, leading to an ultimate acceptance of destiny and thus of the vicissitudes of life itself. So yes, tragedy is often sad, but experience of it on the stage or in a symphony does not (or should not) make you miserable—just the opposite, in fact.

Mahler's first five symphonies all end happily, and Nos. 2–4 deal explicitly (through sung texts) with questions of faith, innocence, and belief in the afterlife, although each approaches the subject from a different angle. But here's the essential point: whenever Mahler wants to treat the specific subject of what happens after death, he requires words to tell his listeners "this is what I'm talking about." Otherwise, how would they know? This may sound obvious, but as it applies to the Sixth Symphony, it presents a real problem, because Mahler explicitly wishes to depict life held in thrall to an inevitable, fateful destiny without the hope of redemption, and he sets himself the extremely difficult task of expressing this clearly in terms of the nonprogrammatic, abstract musical language that he had adopted for these middle-period symphonies (Nos. 5–7).

Mahler himself noted time and time again that his symphonies all have some autobiographical significance for him, perhaps the Sixth most of all. There's that lyrical second subject in the first movement, supposedly representing his wife Alma; the awkward games of Mahler's two children in the trio of the Scherzo; and finally the great struggle in the finale, in which the hero (presumably Mahler himself) supposedly succumbs to three "hammer blows of fate." Now whether or not one accepts the identity of the "Alma" theme or the meaning of those awkward tunes in the Scherzo doesn't really matter, but according to the standard Mahler legend, out of superstitious dread, Mahler himself removed the last, fatal hammer blow from the score, and indeed the two published versions of the symphony reveal this to be the case. The significance of this act gains an even more titillating savor when taken together with the three blows of fate that were soon to befall Mahler: the death of his daughter, the diagnosis of his own heart condition, and his resignation from the Vienna Court Opera. Irresistible, isn't it? And Mahler saw it all in his Sixth Symphony, right? Wrong.

The musical problem Mahler had to deal with in realizing the finale of his Sixth Symphony stems from the simple fact that if indeed the last hammer blow represents death, then what's the rest of the music in the movement for? What does it tell us? How do we know the precise moment of death or that it occurs at all—unless, of course, we look outside the music itself for an explanation? And who in this finale is the hero? What tune or tunes represent him, and what do the others then represent? Most critically, how can music without words convey the answers to these questions all by itself? These are the purely musical questions that Mahler had to address in framing his tragedy in symphonic terms.

Interestingly, the most famous tragedy of all, Sophocles' *Oedipus Rex*, doesn't end in the death of the protagonist (he blinds himself and becomes an exile), and it doesn't need to in order to create the necessary catharsis in its audience. His destiny is not to die, but rather (as everyone knows) to kill his father and marry his mother, and the tragedy lies in the fact that his (and his parents') struggles to avoid this fate in fact precipitate it. This futile attempt to escape fate and the inability to avert inevitable catastrophe (never mind the specific details of plot and character) is something that abstract music can in fact convey very well, through tried-and-true methods of repetition, development, climax, and contrast. Add to these Mahler's own special vocabulary of gestures and motives, and the result is a musical language perfectly able to express the essence of tragedy.

Now let's look at the music itself and try to discover some of the ways in which Mahler produces the necessary catharsis in us, the listeners, by evoking our emotions of pity and terror before the workings of an implacable fate.

First Movement

The symphony begins with a march, grim and determined, constructed around the Mahler rhythm. After a couple of minutes, this first subject disintegrates with a crash on the cymbals and comes to a complete stop. A roll on two snare drums accompanies a simple rhythm played by two timpanists: *dum, dum, dadum, dum, dum* (note that it *contains* the Mahler rhythm). Over this rhythm, a bright major chord on the trumpets turns into a dark minor chord on the oboes. These two ideas—the rhythm and the major chord becoming minor—represent fate.

Even if it weren't known that this was Mahler's intention, it would be pretty obvious, as the two motives never change and always appear later at especially important or dramatic moments, especially in the finale. These recurrences cumulatively suggest very well the idea of predestination, and I will show later how Mahler very obviously constructs the entire finale so as to make this concept particularly clear. Right now, however, the meaning of these motives has yet to be fully revealed.

As the "fate rhythm" fades away, a quiet chorale in the woodwinds (note the bits of the opening march underneath, played by plucked strings) leads directly to a sweeping, lyrical second subject, the tune that the composer's wife Alma claimed described her. It has three parts: a wide-spanning violin theme, a jolly little interlude featuring woodwind, trombones, timpani, and glockenspiel, and then a full orchestral reprise of the violin tune. This rises swiftly to a grand climax and then fades away in contentment.

Most performances then follow Mahler's instructions to return to the symphony's beginning and repeat this opening section. Some on the other hand do not, and this question of observing the repeat is one of those controversial issues that Mahlerian true believers like to get upset about. Aside from the first movement of the First Symphony, this is the only place in all of Mahler that includes a literal exposition repeat. Mahler knew perfectly well that by 1905 all such suggestions had long since been regarded as optional, and he doubtless regarded it so as well.

The development of the movement's main thematic material begins by establishing the significance of that fate rhythm. It swiftly becomes the accompaniment to variations on the opening march themes, amplified by maniacal laughter in the woodwinds and xylophone. Sudden interjections on lower strings of the Alma theme between xylophone cackles lead eventually to an oasis of tranquility: soft strings, celesta, gentle Mahler rhythms in the timpani, and tinkling cowbells offstage create an unforgettable aura, as solo horn and violin spin out lyrical fragments of the second subject. Using the sound of cowbells, like the jester's bells in the Fourth Symphony, is one of the characteristic uses of pure, unpitched noise as a structural tool binding the movements of the symphony together that Mahler pioneered and that later composers took up with such enthusiasm. It's a device as simple as it is imaginative and effective.

A new, more brightly colored march tune interrupts the idyll and brings the listener back to the opening, now more harshly scored than ever. This leads, as at the opening, through the fate motives to a shorter, somewhat less frenetic recapitulation of the Alma theme. As this dies away, soft strokes on the tam-tam herald a resumption of the march-with-fate-rhythm complex from the development, including an outright brutalizing of that jolly little second-subject middle section on trombones and glockenspiel. Suddenly a hush falls over the orchestra, the fragments of the Alma theme gather themselves for a final assault, and in a huge rush accompanied by pounding timpani (Mahler's "motive of celebration"), and as many triangles as there are free hands to play them, her tune concludes the movement in a glorious rush of violins, horns, and trumpets. The very last bars assert the Mahler rhythm obsessively, ending with one last great *dum, dadum* for full orchestra.

Second Movement

Before considering the music of the Scherzo, I need to talk about the order of the two inner movements. Here's the bottom line: Mahler never made up his mind. All that is known is what he did on various occasions, and despite the fact that he revised the score at one point to place the Andante second and the Scherzo third, the general consensus among performers and listeners since his death has been that the symphony works best with the Scherzo second, which is how the symphony's first published edition had it and how many (including those closest to Mahler at the time of his death) believe he wanted it played.

It may very well be, difficult though this is for some to accept, that Mahler wrote a work in which either option is equally viable, and this accounts for his lack of instructions. After all, what matters in terms of the symphony's main argument is the drama of the finale. The Scherzo and the Andante are both mood pieces, not the principal actors in this particular tragedy. The nice thing about recordings, of course, is that you can play the work however you please and see what works best in your own opinion.

So let us turn now to the Scherzo, which is the second movement (for the time being, anyway).

The opening movement's triumph turns out to be short-lived. Once again pounding basses and timpani begin what sounds like a march, only this one has a serious limp. If the tunes remind you of the first movement, they should, because they belong to the same family. In particular, it's not long before the xylophone puts in an appearance with exactly the same sort of music (maniacal laughter) that it played only minutes before. The Scherzo continues in an ominous, lumbering dance until one of the fate motives—the major chord turning minor—forces the music into the middle section (or trio), a grotesque little minuet that Mahler marks "old fashioned" and that never seems to be able to count the correct number of beats. That's because rather than writing it "in three" like a normal minuet, Mahler writes it—more or less—in a rhythm of seven, so the beats never come where you expect them to. There's always one too many or too few. The impression of forced, hollow jollity that this technique produces is really very graphic.

Several times this works itself up into a state of excitement, until the opening timpani rhythm introduces a third section, a grimly sarcastic little dance based on five-note woodwind squeals (you may have heard these preceding the xylophone in the Scherzo proper) and clacking strings struck with the wood of their bows. This leads back to the Scherzo's A section, more frantic than ever, eventually blown to bits by an even more powerfully hysterical eruption of the fate chord. Once again there is the old-fashioned music and the grim little dance, and once again the principal themes of the Scherzo return, until at last a stroke on the tam-tam and a downward rush on the flutes and horns carry the music into the depths. As the music creeps to a close, listen carefully: underneath fragments of the old-fashioned music, you can hear the fate chord turning major to minor, over and over, again and again, until a few quiet taps on the timpani end the nightmare.

Third Movement

If the second movement developed most of the first movement's nastier elements, the third does just the opposite. Here is that distant oasis in the middle of the first movement that we dimly remember, now made real. Although none of the fate motives appear, the way the opening tune keeps moving from major to minor, from luminous to shadowed calm, keeps its presence subconsciously in mind. Essentially, this lovely movement alternates two very long, very beautiful melodies. The first has the character of a lullaby; the second is more urgently passionate. Mahler doesn't reveal this second theme all at once. He interrupts its first appearance, played by the English horn underneath soft harmony in the flutes, with a complete reprise of the lullaby, begun on solo French horn.

Compare this technique to the first movements of the Second and Third Symphonies, where anticipations of music to come also appear briefly, only to be delayed by a return to the music of the respective movements' openings. It's a simple strategy that provides an effective means to enlarge the movement's form through simple repetition (although as always with Mahler, repeats are seldom literal). Only when the second tune comes round again does it unleash a broad torrent of melody, and this leads to a glorious nature scene, as a gently rocking theme in the clarinet, echoing horns, and cowbells in the orchestra make that distant oasis from the first movement a tactile presence. A sort of musical promised land, previously heard only from a distance, has finally been reached.

But the dream dissolves, paradise lost, and the opening theme returns, more disembodied than ever, until this too eventually evaporates. Then, in a magical passage marked *misterioso,* Mahler softly dwells on memories of the pastoral idyll we just experienced. Soft chords on the harp and celesta, murmuring basses, a sweet solo violin, and a gentle *ding* on the triangle create the impression of time standing still. Ever so gently, Mahler returns to the second tune, which suddenly erupts in the violins, this time more urgently than ever.

In the same way that, towards the end of the first movement, Mahler brutalized the second subject's jolly middle section, here he lets the horns maul the clarinet's rocking theme, as cowbells now clash loudly and painfully against the violent return of the opening lullaby. It's a classic example of Mahler's ability to distort what was once calm and lovely, turning it into something angry and wounded. As the music surges on, it finds its way at last to a consoling final cadence, and all passion spent, the movement slowly fades away in melodic fragments to chords on the harp and celesta.

Finale

The dramatic action of this vast finale takes place in four distinct musical zones, each one with its own specific atmosphere characterized by the timbres of the instruments Mahler chooses to emphasize. Three of these we already know. First, there are the march elements, featuring brass and military percussion, including snare drum, triangle, cymbals, rute, and glockenspiel (which takes over from the xylophone in the demonic laughter department). Second, there are the surging lyrical tunes employing violins, sweeping harps, and glorious horns, often thrust forward by rolls on the bass drum. Third, there's the pastoral oasis of cowbells, harps, and celesta. It's important to understand in this connection that although Mahler likes to quote themes from one movement to the next, you don't need to remember them consciously most of the time if you recognize the music by type.

To these musical landscapes Mahler adds a fourth: the "twilight zone," a place of terror and mystery. This new region is the antithesis of the pastoral oasis, just as the lyrical episodes counteract the march passages, and it uses many of the same musical ideas that are associated with peace and tranquility, only distorted and transformed into something frightful. The gentle cowbells become deep bells randomly struck, a magnificently haunted sound. The softly resonant harp has its strings plucked with guitar picks, the celesta now sounds cold and alien, a tuba growls in the depths, and those odd little five-note woodwind squeals from the Scherzo's third section mockingly look on, like crows in a graveyard calling out to each other over the tombstones. And so, this region isn't really that new at all, but rather newly constructed of elements that the listener may recall from elsewhere, even if only subconsciously. That's what gives the music such a strange, half-remembered, nightmarish quality.

This is where the finale begins. A soft thud of the bass drum, a whoosh of cymbals, and through swirling harps, a soaring violin theme reaches upwards, only to be cut off by a stern horn tune that heralds the return of the fate motives, looming out of the orchestral fog exactly as they first appeared way back at the symphony's beginning. This opening violin theme acts almost as a door leading to two different places. Played without the fate motives, it takes the listener to the oasis. Otherwise, as here, the music sinks down into darkness, and the listener enters the twilight zone. Bits of themes float about, punctuated by recurrences of the fate motives, sometimes with their characteristic rhythm, and then just the changing chord by itself. Note especially the solo tuba, harping on the Mahler rhythm over and over. There's some really frightening scoring here: it is, in fact, classic horror movie music, and the most amazing thing about it is that every note anticipates a principal theme of the quick section to which it leads.

Gradually the music gathers speed, until another one of Mahler's powerful marches develops. Once again the Mahler rhythm is very prominent, and the characteristic snare drum rolls, timpani thuds, and cackling laughter (now, as mentioned, on glockenspiel rather than xylophone) are heard. This leads suddenly to an innocent theme on horns and woodwind, and so to a mere foretaste of this movement's lyrical, singing Alma music (even though Mahler never called it that, it has the same function and a very similar sound, so why not make life easy and keep the terminology consistent?) Cut off by a return of the march, Mahler pulls the bottom out from under the orchestra, and the opening returns without the fate motives, leading, as noted above, to the cowbell oasis. Notice once again one of Mahler's favorite techniques, familiar from the slow movement, of giving his listeners a hint of music to come before returning to the previous mood and texture.

As with all the moments of repose in the symphony, this one turns out to be brief. The quiet tinkling of the cowbells yields to the more ominous clash of deep bells, and the marching music makes as if to return. But instead, in a dramatic surprise, it's the Alma tunes that sail in, more radiant than ever before. The violins and horns sweep onward to what seems like a final, fulfilling major cadence, only to have the first hammer blow send the music careening off track. The strings begin a furious march once again, as the brass roar out distorted bits of the lyrical theme like a scream of pain. Eventually these reach a brief plateau of seductive calm (rippling harps and trilling flutes introduced by an ecstatic version of the opening violin theme). Violent brass rudely interrupt, leading to a wild climax, a dramatic pause, and then a crash on the cymbals, a thud on the bass drum, and a smash from the tam-tam as more march music, accompanied by the rute, begins grimly but soon develops into a cheerful little episode.

The import of this development section is very clear: cheerfulness keeps trying to break through the music's angry demeanor. Again the post-hammer-blow fragments of the Alma tunes return on the brass, leading this time to a new version of the violin's opening theme without the fate motives (played upside down, actually), and so we expect to arrive at another oasis. Indeed the music seems headed in that direction, when suddenly the second hammer blow blasts the music into an even more furious maelstrom of raging brass and rushing strings. The orchestra tries to gather itself together but, like an out-of-control train, can't apply the brakes in time to prevent disaster. So with a great crash on the tam-tam, the fate motives return to accompany the violin music of the very opening, and we're back in the twilight zone. The first half of the finale thus ends exactly where it started.

The whole point of this finale's first half is that no matter what the music does, its attempts to resolve happily always fail. The hammer blows fulfill a dynamic function and embody a classic Mahlerian gambit that recurs again and again in his music: the glorious climax that goes wrong and misses its target. But in order to achieve tragedy, Mahler must take this concept a step further. He must show the impossibility of that desired, happy resolution and assert the dominion of fate over all of the actors in his drama. Mahler accomplishes this in two ways in the movement's second half.

First he recapitulates all of the music heard so far in reverse order: oasis, Alma music, and then march, producing an inexorable darkening of tone and texture even as the energy level rises. So listeners begin in the twilight zone, and where once the cowbells yielded to the dark tolling of funeral chimes, here the exact opposite happens. The twilight zone music dissolves into the oasis, and it seems as if the nightmare is finally over. The appearance of the Alma music only adds to this impression, and it reaches a huge climax, racing forward oblivious to the timpani pounding out the fate rhythm as accompaniment. Another climax, and the march music returns for the very last time, more ferocious than ever, but here too the fate motives make their presence felt, the rhythm pounded out on timpani and bass drum.

The Alma music soon adds its own energy to that of the march, and so do all of the movement's other themes, in a magnificent polyphonic development designed to carry all before it. There's even one point where a surprising visitor to this particular drama is encountered: a "special guest appearance" by Mahler's aspiration theme or motive of hope—a two-note descent followed by a rising scale, repeated in ascending sequence. Here it appears in the trumpets, just before the final repetitions of the fate rhythm in the timpani heralding the music's ultimate collapse.

As this titanic battle for resolution proceeds, Mahler's second stratagem becomes clear. The fate rhythm gains in strength and prominence while the orchestra struggles ever more furiously against it. As all of the themes appear in combination, it becomes clear that every single important tune in this movement contains within it this very same fate rhythm: *dum, dum, dadum, dum (dum)*. Even the Alma music (that most of all), even the music from that wonderful plateau of calm heard earlier on—everything boils down to that single, oppressive rhythm. And the moment this is clear, just when the music seems to be headed towards its most radiant apotheosis, a crash on the tam-tam heralds the final collapse, and once again, listeners find themselves back in the twilight zone.

Originally this was the point, at the return of the opening violin music where fate makes its last-but-one appearance, that Mahler placed the third hammer blow. However, unlike the previous two, it does not deflect the music onto another path, nor does it contribute to the final tragic catastrophe (which has just happened a few bars previously). It is in fact musically irrelevant, adding nothing to what is already known, and the most likely reason that Mahler removed it is because the very essence of his scoring is the elimination of all that is superfluous.

But whether it's in or out (and one argument for the other side, in favor of keeping it in, is that it's the only time in the symphony when all of the fate elements come together), the important thing to remember is that Mahler achieves tragedy not by including loud percussive thuds on a hammer or any other instrument but through the design of the themes themselves and the way in which he combines and develops them. What counts is the clarity and inevitability of the unfolding dramatic *process,* not any single specific event or gesture.

But the drama isn't quite over. Now comes the denouement: acceptance of fate's supremacy. The trombones and tuba utter a slow, dark lament based on the opening violin theme, while the horns' repeated, soft descending octaves add their own calm "amen." Mahler's musical door has closed for good; there is nowhere left to go. The music's message couldn't be clearer. As the last vestiges of the movement's opening music trail off into silence with exhausted reiterations of the Mahler rhythm, a sudden, stunning crash presents fate in its most devastating form yet, for above the rhythm of the drums there is no major chord, only the minor. Hope, Mahler seems to say, is an illusion.

There is only fate, and then silence, punctuated by a soft thud on the bass drum.

A more emphatic ending it would be difficult to imagine. Just as the hero of a drama, however noble, has his tragic flaw, so the characters in this symphonic drama carry within them the seeds of their own downfall, a catastrophe that, thanks to Mahler's ability to find musical equivalents for the elements of classical tragedy, produces the necessary catharsis whenever you listen to the symphony.

Symphony No. 7

Mahler's Seventh Symphony, although certainly not as misunderstood or unpopular as it used to be, still often finds itself the object of bewilderment, particularly among those sadly numerous classical-music aficionados who believe that only music expressive of tragedy or misery has true depth and that happy endings can only be achieved after colossal struggles with despair, horror, doubt, and suffering. Mahler's Seventh not only repudiates this point of view, it mocks it, gleefully and unapologetically, and for this it has never quite been forgiven.

The efforts of the miserable many to turn this basically happy, colorful, and often humorous work into yet another "dark night of the soul" start with the nickname "Song of the Night," which Mahler never knew and certainly would never have sanctioned. True, he did call the symphony's second and fourth movements "night music," and he marked the central Scherzo "shadowy." Even so, these three pieces employ the idea of night not for the purpose of inducing dread or an emotionally depressing state but rather in the same way as Chopin's or Debussy's Nocturnes: to evoke moods magical, mysterious, fantastic, nostalgic, and romantic.

It's understandable that, coming hard on the heels of the epic, truly tragic Sixth Symphony, the Seventh should puzzle those looking for more of the same (consider the Fourth Symphony when compared to its more obviously grandiose predecessors) and induce them to attempt to discount and otherwise rationalize away its upbeat mood as hollow or superficial. The only thing superficial in this equation is such people's understanding of Mahler's genius. He can express joy as easily as sorrow, and his wonderful musical sense of humor (the most pointed since Haydn's) still has not received its due in the critical and biographical literature (critics and biographers not being generally the most jolly of listeners). Even in his own lifetime, contemporary critics constantly rebuked Mahler for his music's lack of seriousness and his fondness for grotesque humor. Today they really should know better.

Alas, there will always be those who listen to the Seventh Symphony and aren't amused. Mahler knew it, of course, which is precisely why this piece, its finale in particular, still infuriates some and delights others. Like Beethoven, Mahler understood that the greatest victories are often those won in the common light of day; that catchy dance tunes sound great next to heavenly chorales; that tragedy is meaningless without comedy; and that it's a good thing to toss a little dissonance into the pot now and then, just to keep everyone's ears perked up. The last pages of the symphony mingle the pealing of church bells with the clangor of cowbells. What it all comes down to in the end is a joyful noise, and for those who can't sit back and delight in the cacophony, well, the joke's on them.

Mahler composed his Seventh Symphony in the years 1904 and 1905. It employs a beautifully balanced, five-movement "arch" form (fast–slow–fast–slow–fast) and is scored for a slightly smaller orchestra than the Sixth (particularly in the brass department), but one used in an even more extravagantly colorful and fantastic manner. The list of instruments includes:

- piccolo
- four flutes (fourth doubling second piccolo)
- three oboes
- English horn
- E-flat clarinet
- three clarinets in A and B-flat
- bass clarinet in A and B-flat
- three bassoons
- contrabassoon
- tenor horn in B-flat (a band instrument of the baritone family)
- four horns
- three trumpets
- three trombones
- tuba
- timpani (minimum of four drums)
- triangle
- suspended cymbals
- crash cymbals
- tam-tam
- snare drum
- bass drum with cymbals attached (played by a single musician)
- bass drum
- rute (bundle of sticks slapped against the bass drum case)
- deep bells
- cowbells
- tambourine
- mallet glockenspiel
- keyboard glockenspiel
- two harps
- guitar
- mandolin
- strings

First Movement

The fantastic sound world that Mahler reveals in this symphony starts at the very beginning, as dark string chords accompany the doleful sound of the tenor horn, immediately answered by screeching winds. If you've heard the first movement of Mahler's Third Symphony, you will recognize the heavy death rhythm of the strings as one of the inspirations Mahler adapted from Verdi's operas, while the tenor horn recalls the earlier work's solo trombone. Although, as with the first movement of the Sixth Symphony, Mahler is writing a gigantic example of classical sonata form, he uses a technique adapted from the Fifth Symphony, in which he clarifies the form by identifying certain themes with certain instruments, in this case, brass and strings.

In fact, the easiest way to hear this movement isn't in terms of the vocabulary of sonata form at all (exposition, development, recapitulation), because both here and in the succeeding movements, Mahler takes great pains to create musical structures that are unusually symmetrical. Here, for example, in pyramid form is how this movement lays out as its themes and episodes strike the ear at a first pass:

4. Central "Moonlight" Episode

3. Introduction   5. Introduction

2. Allegro   6. Allegro

1. Introduction   7. Introduction (Coda)

It's certainly interesting that this first movement of the Seventh Symphony has seven sections, symmetrically arranged. Using letters to represent the various sections, the form looks like this: ABACABA.

The music of the introduction quickly arrives at a typically Mahlerian march rhythm in quicker tempo, and under thudding timpani, the trombones announce the movement's principal theme (version 1). If you know the Sixth Symphony's opening movement, you might recognize this tune as a very close relative to its own main theme. A return to the opening tenor horn music, expanded and developed (Mahler almost never repeats himself literally, especially in this symphony), leads into the allegro that dominates the remainder of the movement's musical discourse. Notice the galloping rhythm of the accompaniment, so reminiscent of that most famous Seventh Symphony of all: Beethoven's.

Unison horns now blare out the previous trombone theme, only in an extended form (I'll call it version 2). This leads to a transitional episode for strings and lachrymose horns in alternation, based on a speeded-up development of the tenor horn's music (note the similar rhythm here: *daDum, daDum*), finally arriving at a lyrical second subject, very passionate, given exclusively to the violins. Note the pauses on high notes, the exaggerated dynamics, and the climax that screams more than it soars. This tune believes itself to be the most beautiful melody in the universe, but it comes across more like a dowdy, middle-aged spinster dressed as a sexy young teenager.

Trumpets dismiss this imposter with a return to the opening theme and initiate a vast development of all the previous material, covering a huge amount of musical terrain in a very harsh and "bony" idiom. At what seems to be the height of confusion, with all of the various themes and motives tossed about like ships in a storm, a crash on the cymbals brings the music to a dead halt. Soft trumpets play gentle fanfares, woodwinds add birdcalls based on the omnipresent galloping rhythm, and the cellos intone a soft chorale. It's all music that's been heard before in the introduction, only transformed. American television fans will recognize a trumpet call that sounds amazingly like the opening of the original *Star Trek* signature tune. Ever so gently, the music gathers shape and direction, until an upward sweep from the two harps ushers in an episode of pure romantic beauty—the real thing this time.

It's the second subject, at last appearing in the violins in its ideal form, accompanied by the galloping rhythm softly intoned by horns and winds, with trumpets and trombones solemnly adding the Mahler rhythm in rich chords. Mahler asks that the violins play "without emotion" at first, a direction he reserves for special moments of otherworldly stillness. But passion quickly intrudes on the scene, as brass and percussion take the tune rapidly to its climax. Now the reason for the comparatively high level of surrounding dissonance becomes clear: it's all preparation for this single, special moment, a dream that leads, like so many visions of paradise, to a rude awakening—in the form of a return to the music of the slow introduction.

Trombones now engage the tenor horn in dialogue under the death rhythm of the strings, sounding more than ever like the similar music in the first movement of the Third Symphony. (The tune of the trombone's first entry will actually return as an important woodwind theme at the opening of the Eighth Symphony's second movement.) The darkness builds ominously, with rolls on timpani and bass drum, until a crash on the cymbals announces the return of the quick music on the horns (version 2), more ferocious then ever, with bolder scoring, sharper rhythms, and louder dynamics throughout.

Mahler now reviews all of the principal themes in their original order. The return of the authentic, awkward version of the second subject is particularly interesting: the tune is closer to its original appearance, but the accompaniment (listen to the harps) belongs to its later, transfigured entrance, almost as though it has learned a few cosmetic tricks along the way. Indeed, it almost succeeds in recapturing the serenity of its ideal form, but the full orchestra breaks in wildly and starts a march-tempo coda featuring snare drum, tambourine, and glockenspiel, based on the movement's principal theme (version 1, so marking the final return of the movement's introduction), which quickly brings this fascinating music to a defiantly brilliant major key close with a final assertion of the all-pervasive Mahler rhythm, exactly as in the Sixth Symphony.

Second Movement: "Nachtmusik I" (CD Track 4)

The form of the second movement is really fascinating. Its multiple sections inhabit three distinct tempo areas arranged symmetrically in this pattern: ABABCACBABA. These three tempo areas have the job of displaying for your listening pleasure three corresponding groups of distinct themes and motives. So the whole movement basically looks like this:

A: allegro moderato: horn calls and "birdsong" leading to climax that collapses to the Sixth Symphony's fate motive—a bright major chord dissolving into the minor key

B: andante: the principal march theme (1:24), designated by Mahler as tempo 1

A: horn calls only (5:43), very lonely sounding, with offstage cowbells

B: march theme (6:46) on muted horns

C: *poco meno mosso* (7:46): oboe duet

A: birdsong crescendo (8:42), with fate motive at the movement's center, leading to

C: on two solo cellos this time (9:09), with "tango" accompaniment

B: march again (10:20), now on lower strings with solo flute arabesques and little harp shudders, possibly borrowed from Dvorák's tone poem "The Wood Dove"

A: horn call only, but on trumpet (10:38), clarinet, and flute, effecting a transition back to

B: played by the full orchestra (10:53) as at the beginning, but with greatly enriched scoring

A: expanded birdsong with horn cadenza (15:20), ending on a ghostly fade-out over the fate motive

This may not strike you as thrilling, but it demonstrates how concerned Mahler is in this symphony with symmetrical forms, both within individual movements and as regards the symphony as a whole. It provides further evidence for this being the most classical of his symphonies, in the sense that emotional expression and structure are equally important, carefully balanced, and organized down to the smallest detail. It also offers a special experience that only music can provide, which is that of actually hearing the music's architecture unfolding as it is played.

This doesn't mean that you have to come away from the movement saying, "Wow! What a cool palindrome!" which this piece in fact is. It does mean, though, that you will feel satisfaction as you hear these sections parade before your ears in constantly recurring variations. It's the kind of thing that Haydn and Mozart enjoyed doing, and Mahler has (as usual) taken great pains to make the form extremely clear by creating highly distinctive and varied musical materials that stick in your memory.

Section A

The opening of the second movement features the sound of horns, calling and answering. Woodwinds soon break in (0:33), chirping, trilling, and filling the air with mysterious sounds. A crescendo (1:15) on the rute leads to a miniature climax in the form of a bright major chord turning minor, one of the famous fate motives from the Sixth Symphony, although here purged of all menace. What follows is marvelous.

Section B

The opening horn calls become an unforgettable quiet march (1:24), sliding between major and minor keys, full of growling basses, gurgling bassoons, clacking strings struck with the wood of the bow (1:35), and an occasional loud surprise from the timpani (2:37) in the Mahler rhythm. When the march subsides, a lovely cello tune steals in (3:59), acting as though it wants to become a waltz, but leading always back to the march and ultimately to a perky closing theme (5:00), which tries to end happily but at the last minute slips sternly into the gloom. When it returns in the second half of the movement (13:18), this closing theme has cowbells in the orchestra and little three-note glockenspiel decorations, a sound that a colleague once told me reminds him of a nocturnal festival in Chinatown, with bustling crowds and brightly colored lanterns—a wonderfully apt description.

As the opening horn calls return (5:43), tinkling offstage cowbells add their distinctive touch of loneliness. The march also returns, ghostlike on muted horns, leading to a new theme in the form of:

Section C (7:46)

The tune of this plaintive oboe duet may be new, but it's accompanied by march rhythms and bits of birdsong, so when it arrives, one has the feeling of a new character appearing in familiar surroundings. Ever so gently, other woodwinds add their counterpoints, until the air is full of the buzzing and whirring sounds of the opening (8:42), and that same weird crescendo leads not to the march but back to the oboe duet, here given to the cellos (9:09) with an accompaniment that sounds suspiciously like a tango—no doubt a typically Mahlerian touch of sleazy humor.

These then are the principal actors in this captivating exercise in light and shade. Mahler himself supposedly admitted that the music was inspired by Rembrandt's painting "The Night Watch," but as in most such cases, we must remember that *inspiration* does not mean imitation or illustration. There are also connections between this movement and one of Mahler's very greatest songs: "Revelge" (Reveille), which describes the ghostly marching of a battalion of dead soldiers returning from the grave to reenact old battles in perpetuity. That music can only have come from one source and one composer: Mahler.

Third Movement

The grotesque waltz parody that comprises the "shadowy" (Mahler's indication) third movement lurches about with drunken abandon, its general high spirits continually undermined by bumps, thumps, and scurrying strings. This is basically a new and improved version of Saint-Saëns's famous *Danse macabre,* written in the symmetrical classical form perfected by Beethoven of a scherzo with two trios: ABABA. The A sections consist of bits of rhythm and accompaniment figures that gradually coalesce into an exaggerated dance, one that never manages a smooth ending but continually gets interrupted, falls apart, or trips over itself.

The trio section (B) is another oboe tune, an exercise in fake folk music similar to the tango in "Nachtmusik I." It also belongs to the same general family as the old-fashioned middle section of the Sixth Symphony's Scherzo. This trio has its own contrasting middle section that returns to the mood of the opening waltz (but it's based on the tenor horn tune that opened the symphony, played in the Mahler rhythm). You can't miss it because it leads to the only two cymbal crashes in the entire movement—before returning to the trio's initial oboe theme, now played by strings.

The main waltz slinks back onto the scene, even more skittish and spasmodic than previously, and at one point Mahler asks the basses to pluck their strings so hard that they rebound against the instrument's fingerboard with a resounding *crack!* Right after this the oboe tune interrupts once again, this time amusingly scored for vulgar trombones and tuba, and to fragments of both waltz and trio the music gradually disintegrates exactly as at the end of the Scherzo of the Sixth Symphony (but with none of that movement's sadness), ending with a humorous bump from timpani and pizzicato violas.

Fourth Movement: "Nachtmusik II"

As is proved by the opening of this movement, "Night Music II," evening is also a time for love. Mahler's tempo designation is *andante amoroso,* and if you've ever seen the operas *Don Pasquale, The Barber of Seville, Il trovatore,* or several others, the image of the tenor with lute or guitar offering a nocturnal serenade to his beloved will come to mind when you hear this music. Of course, Mahler's is no mere song under the balcony sort of thing, but a kind of serenade on steroids featuring every plucked instrument he could get his hands on, including harp (sometimes played with a pick), mandolin, and guitar. The full scoring of this exquisite exercise in orchestral chamber music is:

- two flutes
- two oboes
- English horn
- two clarinets
- bass clarinet
- two bassoons
- contrabassoon
- two horns
- two harps
- mandolin
- guitar
- strings

In "Nachtmusik II," Mahler achieves one of the Holy Grails of classical music: the witty slow movement. Listening to this particular charmer, can you imagine a more delicious embodiment of gentle humor in tones?

Since this movement is a stylized love song, Mahler has written it in classic verse-and-refrain song form, albeit with a contrasting middle section. However, this middle section contains a central interlude of its own in a minor key, so the entire movement ultimately has this typically symmetrical structure: ABCBA, and so, like the first Nachtmusik, it's a musical palindrome, although smaller in size, in keeping with its refined atmosphere and chamber music scale.

The A section begins with the refrain on solo violin. This comes back, sometimes on violin, sometimes on cello, and in between are the verses. These consist of variations on a few simple motives: a burbling clarinet tune over strumming guitar, a horn motive featuring three repeated notes, and brief interjections from harps, mandolin, and guitar. Eventually the violins put together a more sustained passage, leading to a brief climax, and this initial section gradually comes to a close while at the same time gently preparing for what happens next.

The middle section (B) is a lovely melody for cello and horn, accompanied by the burbling clarinet figures. This yields to a more passionate string tune, with plaintive interjections from the mandolin (C). The cello/horn tune returns, now on violins, and leads to a heavenly cadence—floating string chords supported by luscious runs in the harp. Mahler now reintroduces the solo violin refrain, and the A section returns in shortened form, leading after only a couple of verses to a dramatic climax that evaporates as if by magic, leaving mandolin and high violins chirping away wittily, oblivious to the passing storm. The last pages get about as close to a sly smile as music can.

Fifth Movement

This always controversial, because always hilarious, finale begins with Mahler's tongue firmly in his cheek. "Allegro ordinario" he writes, serving notice that what's coming is a celebration of the commonplace, the cheap, the tacky, and the vulgar. In other words, it's anything but ordinary. Either you love this music or you hate it. There's no fence-sitting possible. Four timpani bang out a solo fanfare, answered by the brass in the form of a chorale often thought to be a parody of the opening of Wagner's *Die Meistersinger*, but also simply a development of the first movement's principal theme (version 2). This introduces a heroic tune in dialogue between strings, horns, and timpani, building to a triumphant climax of fanfares for trumpets and drums, cut off by a shockingly funny, abrupt modulation to the wrong key—an obvious nose-thumbing at Mahler's own Sixth Symphony major-chord-turning-minor fate motive.

Like the finale of the Fifth Symphony, this movement is a rondo, a structure having the form ABACA, etc. This one, how-ever, is on a particularly huge scale. Its form goes something like this:

introduction   rondo: coda
(timpani and brass)   —   ABaCaBaCABaCaCaDA   —

…making it, structurally speaking, a sort of "rondo from hell," which is of course part of the joke—it could go on forever (and its detractors claim that it does exactly that). Or look at it this way: most classical period rondos last less than five minutes. This one averages around seventeen. But as with everything in this symphony, it's actually very cleverly designed, because it needs to counterbalance the symphonic weight of the imposing first movement in order to provide a satisfying conclusion.

Here are the most important points that you need to be aware of when listening:

1. Episode A usually consists not of the whole opening section (or ritornello) but of the first or second halves of the brass chorale that immediately followed the opening timpani fan-fare (which is why I notate it above as little *a* when it returns in this shortened form).

2. If you look at the letters above indicating the shape of the movement and its various sections, you will see that episode A occurs only three times: at the beginning and end of the

movement and exactly in the center (where it's ultimately blown to smithereens by a crash on the tam-tam).

3. As usual in Mahler, different sections are never literally repeated but are always varied just enough to provide additional interest. There's also a lot of symphonic development and cross-hybridization between sections, particularly through contrapuntal combinations of important themes. So don't worry about it if you recognize the tune from one episode making a brief appearance in the middle of another. That's just part of the fun.

4. On either side of the central appearance of the full ritornello (episode A), Mahler gives us four episodes, but here's a curious fact: although Mahler once again creates an extremely symmetrical overarching form for the movement as a whole, in practice this rondo comes across as a spontaneous, riotous collage that sounds more as though it's being improvised on the spot. This tension between the strict form and the often loony, heterogeneous, and chaotic content makes the whole piece a colossal, cumulative joke on an unprecedentedly large scale, and the humor resides not just in the music with which Mahler fills the various episodes but also in their organization: the form itself becomes funny by virtue of the sudden contrasts and nonsequiturs separating its various sections.

5. The B, C and D episodes also contain some delightful surprises of their own. B starts with a whiff of Léhar's operetta *The Merry Widow*. It turns to a minor key on its second appearance, accompanied by bass drum and clicking of the rute, while on its third time at bat (after the central A section), it morphs into Mahler's most characteristic melodic signature: the aspiration theme, very close in shape to the version in the finale of the Fifth Symphony (see the discussion of that work for details).

6. Episode C is actually a sort of musical "shape shifter," a set of variations and the real practical joker in this particular crowd. It begins as a speeded-up version for violins of the horn/strings/timpani main tune of the opening A section (the theme that comes in after the brass chorale), and this often leads to further variations in the style of "schmaltzy" café or salon music—easy listening if you will. Finally, it turns into something vaguely oriental-sounding: "Turkish" music on unison strings or winds, as Haydn and Mozart knew it, often accompanied by bass drum and cymbals (played by a single player). If you know Mozart's "Turkish Rondo" for piano, then you might detect a certain family resemblance. Mahler really has a blast with this exotic excursion. It comes back loud, soft, fast, slow, and even as a shocking interruption (after a grindingly dissonant climax) in the middle of episode D, which is in fact nothing more than:

7. A dramatic return of the principal theme of the first movement (version 2) in both minor and major key versions, played initially by the horns exactly as first heard. The D episode may in fact be more properly characterized as a contest between the stern first movement theme and the mischievous, irritating, perpetually varied music of C, which interrupts first with its Turkish and then with its schmaltzy versions, until finally, with a sudden crash on the cymbals, Mahler says "Oh, the hell with it!" and launches the last appearance of the A section—the full ritornello.

The grandiose coda is based first on the opening brass chorale and then on the first movement tune, again in the horns, with randomly struck chimes and cowbells making as big a racket as possible all the while. It's simply too over-the-top and garish to be taken entirely seriously. As with the end of the Fifth Symphony, the final bars contain one last orchestral dash for the finish line, held up by a humorous interruption, before cymbals slam home the final chord in perhaps the greatest parody of the romantic grand finale in musical history.

There's one additional significant point: the first movement itself ended not with the main theme of its allegro section but rather with version 1 from the movement's introduction. So it's no accident that Mahler reserves version 2 for this finale, closing the very last potential loophole in what is without question the most minutely organized musical structure that he ever built. And just in case any more evidence was needed of Mahler's delight in formal balance and symmetry at every level in this symphony, here's a last little fun fact: music from the opening movement occurs not just here, at the symphony's end, but also (as we have heard) in the Scherzo—in other words, at the symphony's beginning, at its end, and as the middle section in the middle part of the symphony's middle movement.

The Seventh Symphony stands at the opposite pole from the tragic Sixth, a testament not only to Mahler's sanity and fundamentally positive outlook on life but also to his powers of creative self-renewal. Few composers have ever managed to sound at once so much like themselves and so different from one work to the next. Using many of the same ideas that populate the Sixth Symphony, Mahler transforms them and presents them in a vivid new light, showing that tragedy and comedy are two sides of the same coin. Even more than the Sixth, the Seventh constitutes Mahler's tribute to the classical style and, above all, to that period's special delight in pressing into service highly intellectual or learned formal and stylistic devices (such as sonata form, counterpoint, and variation) for no greater purpose than that of providing fabulously witty entertainment.

Symphony No. 8

ahler's Eighth Symphony, composed in 1906, has enjoyed steadily increasing popularity since its 1910 premiere in Munich. Perhaps it was the nickname "Symphony of a Thousand" (which Mahler disliked and did not invent) that prevented its early acceptance. In any event, the piece works perfectly well with half that number of performers, and any major symphony orchestra with a large chorus and capable children's choir can put it on with little difficulty (assuming they have a big enough hall!) Mahler intended his Eighth to be approachable in the broadest possible sense. It has great climaxes, beautiful tunes, and glittering orchestration, and it's the first major symphony ever to be written completely as a vocal work.

The inspired idea of combining the medieval hymn "Veni, creator spiritus" with the final redemptive scene from Goethe's *Faust* perfectly illustrates one aspect of Mahler's belief system: that the religious doctrine of spiritual redemption and Faust's salvation through striving (an ideal embodied in Goethe's concept of the "Eternal Feminine") are merely two sides of the same coin. In the Eighth Symphony, Mahler sets out to prove this concept musically.

The symphony requires:

Onstage:
- two piccolos (several to each part)
- five flutes (flute five plays first piccolo)
- four oboes
- English horn
- E-flat clarinet (doubled throughout)
- three clarinets in B-flat and A
- bass clarinet in B-flat and A
- four bassoons
- contrabassoon
- eight horns
- four trumpets
- four trombones
- tuba
- timpani (two players)
- triangle
- three cymbals (both suspended and crashed)
- bass drum
- tam-tam
- deep bells in A and A-flat
- glockenspiel
- celesta
- piano
- harmonium
- organ
- two harps (several players to each part)
- mandolin (several players to the part)
- strings

Offstage:
- four trumpets (first part with several players)
- three trombones

In addition:
- eight soloists
- two mixed choirs
- children's choir

That's quite a crowd, but as always with Mahler, the sounds he creates are as noteworthy for their refinement, sensitivity, and subtle color as for the overwhelming volume of the big climaxes.

Part I: "Hymnus"

The structure of the symphony follows the general layout of the words: there are two texts by two different authors in two different languages, and therefore just two big movements. However, just as Mahler juxtaposes these particular texts to demonstrate a philosophical similarity between them, so he organizes the music to drive home their relationship to one another. This means that all of the music that you hear in the first movement (which Mahler called part 1) will return in the second (part 2). So rather than get into a pointlessly detailed discussion of form in the abstract, all you really need to do to understand how the symphony works musically is pay special attention to the major tunes and motives in part 1 and the words they illustrate. For convenience's sake, I'll focus on seven:

1. *The opening triumphant cry of "Veni, creator spiritus" (Come, creator spirit):*
   The basses rumble, a blast from the organ, and Mahler launches the symphony at full throttle with the two choirs united in celebration. Notice that both the opening line of text and the brass answer contain the Mahler rhythm, which

will turn out to be the glue that binds the whole symphony together. The other really important motive, one that will soon take on a life of its own, consists of the chorus's first three notes (and those of the brass answer).

2. *The soprano solo, "Imple superna gratia" (Fill them with grace), particularly associated with the women in part 2:*
This lyrical section features the soloists, then the choir, then the soloists once again, and it leads back to the movement's opening. This reaches a huge climax, capped by a majestically tolling bell that gradually imposes a somber, mysterious calm.

3. *The chorus, "Infirma nostri corporis" (Our weak flesh), and following the quirky orchestral interlude with bell sounds to which it leads, also the bass solo on the same words:*
Now things begin to get interesting. The orchestral interlude (about two minutes long) that cuts off the "Infirma" chorus, with its tolling bell and jagged interjections, hammers home two basic ideas: the Mahler rhythm and the three-note leaping motive. This motive in turn becomes the source of the bass solo that follows, leading to the first appearance of the words "Accende lumen sensibus" (Illuminate our senses), although not in that order. The first word is *lumen* (light), and indeed the orchestration is as airy and delicate as Mahler can make it, with high violin lines enrobing the soloists' entreaties.

4. *The huge unison cry of "Accende lumen sensibus" (after its first gentle statement by the soloists) and:*

5. *The first solo entrance of the children's choir immediately afterward with the words "amorem cordibus" (love in our hearts):*
Notice the important pause on the first word: "A—[pause]—ccende." The significant part of the tune begins on its second

note. More to the point musically, this motive is an old friend: the aspiration theme as it first appeared for the very first time in Mahler's work, as the motive of resurrection in the finale of the Second Symphony. Remember the shape of this tune, a two-note drop followed by a rising scale and another drop. It will become very important in part 2. Similarly, the music of the children's chorus will assume even greater importance in the symphony's second part.

6. *The fierce shout of "Hostem repellas longius" (Drive the enemy far away from us):*
   This very important idea will undergo some wonderful and surprising transformations. The rhythm of the first six notes is even more important than the actual tune and is itself derived from the children's singing of "amorem cordibus."

   In the ensuing fugue, a grand passage of complex counterpoint in Mahler's favorite vigorous march tempo, you will hear all of the themes and motives revealed so far juxtaposed, combined, and developed, and from this point on, there really is no new thematic material in the first movement. The fugue runs for several minutes and rises to a huge, dissonant climax (capped by a crash on suspended cymbals) that self-destructs in classic Mahlerian fashion. Anguished cries of "lumen" grope upwards until, on summoning the word "spiritus," the music at last achieves the return of the opening, "Veni, creator spiritus." This leads to a much-shortened recapitulation of the movement's opening themes and episodes, reaching a climax that dies away on:

7. *The major-key (and most important) version of the leaping three-note motive, now played by French horns:*
   This forms the basis for the concluding "Gloria," sung first by the children and then the solo sopranos, and eventually even pounded out by the timpani. If you were listening carefully,

you might have noticed it earlier, just before the previous choral climax when the tenor sings the words "Dissolve litis vincula" (Resolve our strife). The movement ends with great choral shouts of "Gloria Patri" (Glory to the Father) as the offstage brass (usually positioned in an upper balcony) play the aspiration theme against rising scales in the voices. If this doesn't send a shiver down your spine, then you're probably close to dead.

Finally, notice the importance of the Mahler rhythm as the music proceeds. This is the rhythm that characterizes such words as *spiritus*, *sensibus*, *caritas*, *cordibus*, *gratia*, *Gloria*, *praevio*—any big concept or action word that Mahler wishes to emphasize and imprint on the listener's mind—and he'll do it again throughout part 2. This three-note rhythm also completes the important six-note motive beginning with the words "Hostem repellas," mentioned above. Mahler does not expect you to understand Latin (especially in the jumbled-up form in which he presents the words here), and it's just for this reason that he makes sure to emphasize the important bits of the text whose melodies and motives will figure prominently in part 2. His real goal in part 1 is simply to knock your socks off with the biggest, most glorious noise that he knows how to make, and there's no question that he does just that.

Part 2: Closing Scene from Goethe's Faust

Although part 2 recalls or develops music heard earlier, one mustn't lose sight of the fact that just as much of it is original and new. Mahler surrounds the music of part 1 with new material, or new developments of old material, so that whenever he recalls something heard previously in a more or less literal manner, it stands out clearly in contrast to its surroundings.

Part 2 begins with a lengthy orchestral prelude. The opening is magical: a soft swoosh on the cymbals and a high string tremolo, followed by plucked lower strings playing a stark, bare-bones version of "Accende lumen sensibus"—in other words, the aspiration theme. Note how Mahler breaks it up this time: two descending notes, a pause, and then its rising phrase (which is about to take on a life of its own). Next the winds play the "spiritus" rhythm, followed by the same rising phrase in longer notes. The opening *swoosh* is another one of those simple Mahlerian musical gestures, often featuring the sound of percussion, with which Mahler instantly conjures up some special mood.

This, then, is the entire foundation on which Mahler constructs his slow introduction to the last scene of Goethe's *Faust*. Its overall form is ABACBDA. B consists of loud meditation on the "amorem cordibus" theme from the first movement. C is a much more passionate, even wild, interlude for the violins that will shortly become the basis of the tormented aria sung by the character known as "Pater profundus" (bass solo). This leads back to the music of B, and towards the end, you might notice a sudden hush while the winds play D, an archaic-sounding chorale that also begins with the spiritus rhythm.

The brass take up the chorale for a moment, only to be banished with a loud cymbal crash, and when the opening music returns for the last time, the chorus enters against it and sets the scene (literally: the chorus describes the landscape in which the action takes place) in a broken rhythmic monotone. This introductory chorus, which doubles as a complete reprise of the introduction's A section, ends with a two-line chorale consisting entirely of the six-note theme (number 6 above) twice repeated, although differently harmonized. Note the words "Holy place of sacred love."

The mood brightens, and "Pater ecstaticus" (baritone solo) expresses his desire to be purified in the light of divine love. The music consists almost entirely of the same six-note Hostem repellas tune. It is, in fact, a development—or perhaps better expressed, a refinement—of that concept. Where the initial cry in part 1 asks the creator to "Drive the enemy far from us and grant us continual peace," Mahler (and Goethe) here identify the enemy, through the same music, as anything that comes between the soul and direct experience of divine love.

Surging forward, the orchestra begins a turbulent accompaniment to the bass aria of Pater profundus (an extremely difficult piece of singing, incidentally, which requires a huge voice steady over its entire range if it is to dominate the instrumental part). Most of the music is new to this movement, developed from the introduction's episode C as previously mentioned, except when the soloist expresses his desire for "almighty Love," which appears in the form of the rising "Accende lumen sensibus" tune—the aspiration theme.

Suddenly, the mood brightens yet again and the chorus of angels bursts in with a literal quotation of the "Accende lumen sensibus" theme, interrupted by the Chorus of Blessed Boys singing an equally lighthearted version of "Hostem repellas" (which, you may recall, originally derived from their own singing of "amorem cordibus" in the first movement). This quickly evolves into a new, very catchy folk tune played on winds and muted trumpet, shot through with that emphatic spiritus rhythm.

Now comes a lovely interlude sung by the younger angels ("Jene Rosen") that contains an important new theme at the words "Fühlten Liebesqual die Geister" (The spirits felt the pangs of love). Notice that the important music always involves some aspect of the love idea. The interlude concludes with the words "Jauchzet auf!" (Rejoice!) sung to the spiritus rhythm and leads to a contrasting chorus ("Uns bleibt ein Erdenrest") for the lower voices, set to the "Infirma nostri corporis" music from the first movement.

The sense of both texts is similar: the acknowledgment of mortal frailty and weakness and the plea for healing strength that comes only from the spirit of the creator. An alto solo adds her voice to the musical texture, which yields to the entry of the younger angels in quicker tempo, singing the archaic chorale that concluded the orchestral introduction. As the excitement increases, the boys join in with their folk tune, and under it all, the voice of Doctor Marianus (tenor) gradually emerges, singing his paean of praise to the Queen of Heaven (in theory the Virgin Mary, but Goethe never gets quite that specific; rather, he focuses on Mary as the idealization of the Eternal Feminine, "Mater gloriosa" (the Glorious Mother) who is the goal of all masculine striving and the ultimate source of peace and love).

The chorus joins Doctor Marianus in his homage, at the end of which "Accende lumen sensibus" appears briefly in the orchestra, and all of the harps enter in order to introduce a new orchestral interlude, delicately scored for harps, harmonium, and violins. This reduced ensemble plays a tune that might very well be called the "Theme of the Eternal Feminine." A vision of Mary appears (Goethe's Mater gloriosa), and the next sections, including the "Chorus of Penitent Women," three individual soprano and alto solos, and a delightful trio for the three ladies, are all based on completely new music. The women present the case for the redemption of Faust's soul, recalling their own experiences as sinners who have found salvation. This lengthy passage of new music is necessary because with the entrance of "Una Poenitentium" (Gretchen, the woman who Faust seduced and abandoned in earthly life), Mahler begins to tie the musical knot, recalling all of the most significant themes from both parts of the symphony.

First, Gretchen asks Mater gloriosa to look with favor on her plea for Faust's redemption, and Mahler sets the text to a speeded-up version of the Eternal Feminine theme. Listen to the delicate accompaniment, with celesta, mandolin, and piano all adding piquant colors to the orchestral fabric. Gretchen's plea is taken up and amplified by the Blessed Boys (the "Fühlten Liebesqual die Geister" music noted above introduces their chorus), eventually singing for the third and last time their characteristic folk song. Gretchen interrupts them once again, this time uniting her request for grace with the identical musical thought from the first movement: "Imple superna gratia." This rises to a vocal climax (from the words "Und aus ätherischem Gewande") at which, for the first time, the "Veni, creator spiritus" tune returns as well, giving an additional eloquence and a sense of impending triumph to Gretchen's address. At last, to the delicate sounds of the Eternal Feminine theme, the Mater gloriosa delivers her exquisite summons to her followers (a thrilling single line of music for high soprano), telling them to complete the process of redemption of Faust's soul.

Doctor Marianus returns, introducing a chorus celebrating the achievement of divine salvation. The words "Blicket auf" (look upwards) are set to the spiritus rhythm and reverberate through the voices and instruments, with the organ returning for the first time since the first movement to add additional solemnity to this gorgeous hymn. The chorus reaches its climax and subsides, while the orchestra continues to develop the "Blicket auf" theme with increasing excitement, leading to another literal quotation from the first movement: the three-note leaping theme of the "Gloria." Once this quiets down, an ethereal interlude for solo piccolo, harps, piano, celesta, harmonium, and light touches of color from select other instruments introduces the final chorale.

The tune of this chorale unites all of the love themes that have been heard so far. It consists simply and miraculously of four repetitions (each taking in two lines of text and differently harmonized) of the Hostem repellas theme combined with the rising phrase of "Accende lumen sensibus." It thus incorporates the spiritus rhythm as well and represents the fulfilled development of the shorter, embryonic version ("Holy place of sacred love") sung at the end of the introduction to part 2. We can only marvel at the naturalness and inevitability with which Mahler introduces the symphony's moral: Worldly things are but parables, images of a deeper spiritual reality to which the love and grace of the Eternal Feminine summon us.

As the chorale rises to its climax, other significant tunes join in. The Eternal Feminine appropriately appears at the cries of "Ewig, ewig" (Forever, forever), and after a last appearance of the chorale, intoned by all of the voices at full volume and accompanied by the organ, the music comes full circle: the off-stage brass announce "Veni, creator spiritus," while the percussion and trombones hammer home Gloria, and it is this motive that has the last word, twice repeated in long notes, capped by tremendous crashes on cymbals and tam-tam in an ending that harks back to that of the Second Symphony, Mahler's other triumphant assertion of the redemptive power of divine love.

Das Lied von der Erde (The Song of the Earth)

In his Eighth Symphony, Mahler applied techniques of thematic and motivic development to demonstrate (musically) what he believed to be the shared philosophical basis between Western religion and Goethe's humanistic world view. In *Das Lied von der Erde,* Mahler explores the possibility of "symphonizing" the other great preoccupation of his musical life, the song cycle. I have discussed throughout these essays the fruitful cross-fertilization between song and symphony that characterizes Mahler's work. Some symphonies include whole songs or even grew out of them (Nos. 1–4). Others merely make occasional reference to them in passing (Nos. 5, 7, 9, and 10). Now the practice can be seen in reverse, the symphonic principal shaping the process of song composition rather than the other way around, and so leading to the birth of a new hybrid form, the song-symphony.

There's no question that Mahler's selection of texts from Hans Bethge's collection of free German adaptations of oriental poetry, called *The Chinese Flute*, struck a sensitive chord given the tragic events that had overtaken him: the death of his daughter and the diagnosis of his own heart condition. Biographers in love with the biblical number three also like to include his resignation from the Vienna Court Opera in this list of bad things, but this strikes me as opportunistic. As the most famous conductor in the world, Mahler had no lack of job offers, and he was indeed happily on his way to New York to earn more money than ever before leading both the Metropolitan Opera and the New York Philharmonic hardly before the ink was dry on his letter of resignation, so there's no need to inflate the misery index. Losing a child was tragedy enough, I should think.

In these circumstances, it's not surprising that these poems, with their emphasis on the fragility of life, the transience of youth and beauty, and (let us not forget) the perpetual renewal of nature in springtime, spoke with special force to Mahler. That said, the evidence of our ears supports the view that the problems that Mahler addressed in the composition of *Das Lied von der Erde* were musical ones first and foremost. However emotionally necessary this work may have been for him in that terrible summer of 1908 when he wrote most of it, what he in fact does is apply the lessons learned in the composition of the Eighth Symphony to this new musical challenge, coming up with fresh solutions in the process.

Das Lied von der Erde, described as "a symphony for alto (or baritone) and tenor solos and large orchestra," is universally admired for its perfect marriage of text and music, and especially for its remarkable orchestration, which includes:

- piccolo
- three flutes (third flute alternating on piccolo)
- three oboes (one alternating on English horn)
- E-flat clarinet
- three B-flat clarinets
- bass clarinet in B-flat and A
- three bassoons (third alternating on contrabassoon)
- four horns
- three trumpets in B-flat and F
- three trombones

- tuba
- timpani
- glockenspiel
- triangle
- suspended cymbals
- crash cymbals
- bass drum
- tam-tam
- tambourine
- celesta
- mandolin
- two harps
- strings

Since the best way to listen is simply to sit down with the words and follow them as they are sung, and since the job of the music is to support the meaning of the text, there's no need to treat each of the songs in detail. Instead, I'm going to pay special attention to matters of form and to Mahler's treatment of the orchestra. This last item is especially important, because each song uses a different complement of instruments, and just knowing who will be playing says a lot about where the focus of attention should be when listening.

First Movement: "Das Trinklied vom Jammer der Erde" (The Drinking Song of the Earth's Misery)

What a juicy title! This is the only song to use all three trumpets, which, along with the horns, set the musical events in motion. The other major players in this eight-minute drama of bitterness and despair are the flutes (often playing tremolos through the technique known as *flutter-tonguing*), and the glockenspiel, which has some very important solo work. Surprisingly absent, considering the music's turbulence, are the timpani and tuba. The resulting impression is one of great vehemence but without heaviness, none of which makes matters any easier for the tenor, who needs a huge voice and lots of stamina to characterize the text adequately and carry over the big climaxes.

This song has four verses, 1, 2, and 4 ending with the refrain "Dunkel ist das Leben, ist der tod!" (Dark is life, is death!) Verse 3 is a quiet interlude that functions much like the development section of a movement in sonata form. Indeed, the entire song really does have the shape of a classical symphonic first movement: there's an exposition that even gets repeated (verses 1 and 2), a development (verse 3), and a recapitulation (verse 4), followed by a short coda. The first entry of the violins right at the beginning is also very important. They play a three-note descending motive in long notes, then repeat it in short ones. This motive (defined by the notes A, G, and E in the key of the opening) appears throughout the work, not always obviously, as the symphonic glue that binds the various movements together. You can also hear it as the big glockenspiel solo at the beginning the second verse (before the voice enters). Mahler takes great pains to repeat this over and over throughout the movement, because this first song, aside from minding its own business, establishes what will turn out to be the musical continuity of the entire symphony.

The song's development section, verse 3, is particularly important. It begins with the three-note motive in muted trumpet and continues with a long passage for the violins in their upper register, the kind of writing that will return in the finale. Indeed, the melody of the tenor's entrance at the words "Das Firmament blaut ewig" (The firmament is eternally blue) will return to round off the entire work to words added by Mahler that paraphrase the text of this very verse. This accounts for the fact that Mahler sets it off as an oasis of peace amidst the movement's tempestuous outer verses, and once again we see the music having a dual function, as a development of what we have heard thus far (the opening horn call in particular) and also as a foreshadowing of things to come.

Finally, there is the movement's remarkable climax, the terrifying, moonlit image of an ape howling atop the gravestones, taking the tenor to the threshold of musical expressionism as Mahler demands that the voice collapse downwards along with the rest of the orchestra to one of his classic scream (voice), crash (cymbals) and thud (bass drum) combinations. The very ending of the song exploits a last scream in the winds with a final, brutal thud from trombones, low strings, horns, and low woodwinds. You can hear very clearly that this opening features many of Mahler's most characteristic gestures and orchestral fingerprints, establishing at once the work's symphonic formal credentials.

Second Movement: "Der Einsame im Herbst" (The Lonely Man in Autumn)

The remarkably sparse orchestration of this song consists primarily of two flutes, one oboe, two clarinets, bass clarinet, two bassoons, four horns, and strings (without double basses). At the movement's climax, Mahler brings in for just a few bars the basses, two harps, a second oboe, and the third bassoon. Even these numbers are deceptive, for the principal player in this movement is the single oboe, whose solos color the music just as the solo horn colors the Scherzo of the Fifth Symphony or the offstage posthorn characterizes the third movement of the Third Symphony. The oboe's opening three notes in fact spell out the symphony's three-note motto, while the violins wander aimlessly below.

I have shown in previous symphonies how a musical idea in Mahler, used for a structural purpose (that is, to excite your memory of a previous passage and so to relate the two in your mind), may not necessarily be a repeated theme or motive. In this case, what Mahler wants you to remember is the idea of long solos for oboe (and later flute). These images of loneliness will return to haunt the finale, and even though the music will be quite different, the concept and context will be identical.

Third Movement: "Von der Jugend" (Of Youth)

This is the most "Chinese" sounding movement in the entire piece, scored for piccolo, two flutes, two clarinets, two oboes, two bassoons, four horns, one muted trumpet, triangle, cymbals, bass drum, and strings. There has always been a certain "oriental" strain in Mahler's music: Leonard Bernstein in his video *Young People's Concerts* referred to the famous unison passage for four flutes in the first movement of the Fourth Symphony as "Chinese music," and I have shown how certain passages in the Seventh and Eighth Symphony, especially those featuring mandolin, also have something of this character.

This particular example has some interesting features, not least the music's artificiality and brittleness. Mahler isn't trying to convince the listener that this is "real Chinese." Just the opposite in fact: it's like that odd pagoda china cabinet or hideous Oriental lampshade in your grandmother's 1950s living room. Mahler's chinoiserie is in fact the perfect vehicle to illustrate the text, which describes a party of friends in a pavilion of porcelain drinking and chatting—and in doing so, to capture the shallowness and frivolity of youth.

Once again the woodwinds lead (first oboes, then flutes, as in the second movement), and while you won't hear the symphony's motto in any obvious way, it's buried in both the accompaniment and the vocal line. Note the delicate use of bass drum and cymbals and the chugging rhythmic accompaniment of bassoons and horns, one of the clichés that Mahler borrowed from Italian opera. The music at the words "in dem Pavillon aus grünem" shares a strong kinship to the Seventh Symphony's equally stylized "Nachtmusik II" (mandolin solo) and, curiously, the coda to the finale of the Fifth Symphony. In other words, there's more of Mahler than there is of China in this music.

Fourth Movement: "Von der Schönheit" (Of Beauty)

This movement, which opens with gentle birdsong on the flutes, shares a similar message and style with its predecessor and can be seen as complimentary. You may hear the three-note motto in the woodwind tune that accompanies the voice on its first entrance. Fascinatingly, this song uses the largest orchestra of all. Everyone participates (except the third trumpet, celesta, and tam-tam) in the huge central outburst depicting dashing youths galloping by on horseback, the opening of which sounds—I am sure coincidentally—like a bit of Tchaikovsky's *1812 Overture*. Then again, who knows? It could very easily be a Mahlerian in- joke. In any case, the tuba plays only a single phrase in the whole work, the violent minor-key return (on the brass) of the woodwind tune containing the three-note motto, while timpani are restricted to the rhythmic pounding that always means joy or celebration in Mahler's music.

Once the central storm blows over, you will certainly smile at the gentle humor of the coda, the violins refusing to let the music go, stretching it out with their repeated notes until the winds interrupt with the finale chord. This is the most delicate and refined music that Mahler knows how to write, and if the musical moral of the third movement is that youth is superficial and short-lived, what Mahler describes here is the idea that fragile beauty lusts after its own destruction, just as the young maidens in this song yearn for the handsome horseback riders who trample underfoot the garden in which they are sitting and plucking lotus blossoms.

Fifth Movement: "Der Trunkene im Frühling" (The Drunkard in Spring)

All of the woodwinds participate in this jolly song, but only four horns and a single trumpet from the brass, one harp, a triangle, and the strings. This tipsy music admirably illustrates the drunken bravado of the tenor, whose final line, "What do I care about spring? Let me be drunk!" tells you all you need to know about the message of this amusing little movement, with its central dialogue between a singer and a bird (which the drunkard of the title thinks that he can understand, of course).

Mahler peppers this movement with descending three-note phrases, all of which sound derived from the motto, and indeed they are. You can hear it most tellingly in the solo violin at the words "Ich frag' ihn, ob shon Frühling sei" (I ask him whether it's already spring), "him" being the little bird of the above conversation. You may also note that these three-note phrases often occur in the Mahler rhythm and that this rhythm and those three-note motives increasingly take over the vocal line after the calm central episode.

Aside from the music's humor, it contains (as does the fourth movement) one very important musical image that will reappear in the finale: that of birdsong. So although it's very short, this movement actually accomplishes quite a bit symphonically speaking, offering a sort of mini-summing-up of some important motives and Mahlerian trademarks before moving on to the epic finale, which is as long as all of the previous songs put together.

Sixth Movement: "Der Abschied" (The Farewell)

The most characteristic instrument in this movement is the tam-tam, which actually has an extensive solo at one point. Its mysterious and menacing sound colors Mahler's entire orchestral palette. Aside from the tam-tam, the only other percussion involved is the equally dark bass drum. Trumpets and tuba have no place here, but the three trombones play a very important role, and everyone else participates, with especially important solos for flute, oboe, and the harps. At the very end, the celesta makes its single critical appearance in the symphony as well.

More importantly, this finale (which lasts for about thirty minutes) summarizes all of the work's previous content, and it's this symphonic purpose that is of greatest concern. An outline of the movement, with letters representing the music of the various sections, looks like this: ABACBDABACD. As you can see, the music falls into two almost identical halves (the first half has an extra B, but then the next return of A is greatly enlarged in the movement's second half and so more than makes up the difference). Formally speaking, the music resembles a rondo, but the truth is that Mahler has created his own form here in response to both the text and his ultimate intentions for the symphony's conclusion.

Here's a brief description of each section, keyed into the above formal scheme:

A. Opening thuds on the tam-tam, low harps, double basses, and contrabassoon introduce an oboe, playing a melodic turn that gradually expands into a lonely melody in funeral march rhythm, reminiscent of the same instrument's solo in the second movement, only more somber.

B. The singer recites her (or his if the less frequent—and less desirable—baritone alternative is used) opening in duet with the solo flute, under a single long-held note in the cellos. The flute finishes by itself.

A. Low harps lead off, as clarinets and then horns put together a rhythmic figure consisting of three repeated notes and two, two-note falling phrases. In character it recalls the chugging accompaniment on bassoons from the third movement's central section. Over this, the solo oboe introduces the voice. Notice the liquid accompaniment in the harps. As with its first appearance, this passage gently disintegrates in falling scales on contrabassoon, flutes, and cellos.

C. Harps and clarinets play a rocking figure (it will come back in the finale of the Ninth Symphony), over which the oboe sings yet another lengthy solo. When the voice enters again, the flute takes over the oboe's music. The music rises twice to a climax over the next few minutes, leading to a remarkable page of birdsong and then to stillness, as harps and bass clarinet lull the world to sleep ("Die Welt schläft ein!")

B. Flute and voice once again interweave in dialogue over a single note in the basses (instead of the cellos).

D. Now comes the apotheosis of the symphony's three-note motto. Mandolin and harps play a pattern of descending three-note phrases, over which the flute enters with the motto, only now rising (or *inverted* in musical terminology). This introduces a long melody in the violins, the cousin to the tune that characterized the first movement's third verse. Voice and orchestra rise to an ecstatic climax on the words "trunkne Welt!" (drunken world). This suddenly collapses back into the music of the opening.

A. The tam-tam returns, even more menacingly than at the movement's beginning, and with it comes the funeral march, now for orchestra alone, evolving into an extended interlude (about five minutes or so). Above the march rhythm, Mahler's woodwind section sings one of those Jewish/Slavic melodies that he always uses to express heartbreak and longing. (You may hear a curious resemblance between this tune and "Anatevka" from *Fiddler on the Roof*. Both melodies share the same roots and, perhaps not coincidentally, express a nostalgic longing for home.) The funeral march rises to an intense climax, with keening winds wailing above the melody in the violins, coming to rest in a devastating return of the opening tam-tam thuds, now backed by trombones, loud and terrifying.

B. Under a held note in cellos and basses (a nice symbolic touch, using both this last time around), the soloist has her final recitation, only now there's no solo wind to accompany her, only random strokes of the tam-tam. It doesn't get any darker than this.

A. The funeral march returns for a last time as the singer tells of her desire to seek peace for her lonely heart.

C. The English horn has the rocking accompaniment formerly given to harp and clarinet (they take over once the voice begins), while violins have the oboe's melody. The mood brightens in expectation of the singer's journey home at last, and as the violins rise higher and higher, the voice soars in with:

D. The final climax. As mentioned previously, the words are Mahler's, and they paraphrase the first movement's third verse, as does the music. "The dear earth all, over all, blooms again in spring and becomes green again. And forever,

forever, shines the blue horizon, forever, forever.... " As the voice repeats the word "forever" *(ewig)* to falling two-note phrases, harp and celesta play rippling arabesques, the mandolin contributes isolated notes, the flutes play the inverted three-note motto, and trombones sound the final chord as softly as possible while the English horn adds a touch of dissonance. It's hard to believe that such a complete symphonic summation is actually happening in a passage that apparently consists of so little. That final chord never in fact resolves: the music simply stops, poignant and unfulfilled.

Coming hard on the heels of the Eighth Symphony, *Das Lied* tempts listeners to read into it primarily the sadness and disillusionment that Mahler must have felt at this time in his life, but that would probably be a mistake. After all, the work ends with arguably the most serenely beautiful music that Mahler ever wrote. It is also clear that Mahler held fast to his symphonic ideal despite the tragic events of the previous year, and found a way to express his feelings in a manner consistent with his achievements and beliefs as a musician first and foremost. The music's value lies in the fact that it does not represent a break with the past, but instead continues the lines of development that Mahler had been pursuing all along. That he was able to complete it when he did makes its composition one of the truly heroic acts of creative genius.

Symphony No. 9

This symphony, the last that Mahler completed, was composed in 1908–09. Mahler never heard it. Like its immediate predecessor, *Das Lied von der Erde,* with which it shares some of its motives, it expresses a great deal of sadness and resignation; indeed, it is Mahler's darkest symphony after the Sixth, but like that work, the impression it leaves on most listeners is not in the least bit depressing. Rather, the music bespeaks a heightened awareness of beauty and innocence, and only reluctantly (very reluctantly) lets go, in a finale whose last pages, as Leonard Bernstein astutely observed, come as close to describing the experience of dying peacefully as music ever has.

Mahler scored the work for the following typically full orchestra:

- piccolo
- four flutes
- four oboes (fourth alternating on English horn)
- E-flat clarinet
- three clarinets in B-flat and A
- bass clarinet
- four bassoons (fourth alternating on contrabassoon)
- four horns

- three trumpets
- three trombones
- tuba
- timpani (two players)
- bass drum
- snare drum
- four deep bells
- triangle
- glockenspiel
- suspended cymbals
- crash cymbals
- two harps
- strings

The overall structure of the Ninth is very unusual and interesting. Two slow movements flank two quicker ones, but the thematic connections between the symphony's parts suggest yet another of Mahler's symmetrical formal structures: a slow-fast first half counterbalanced by its mirror image, a fast-slow second half. Mahler's orchestration here, as in *Das Lied von der Erde,* reaches a new level of clarity and refinement, so much so that the thought that he never actually heard the music comes as something of a shock.

Mahler himself pointed out that the previous symphony that comes closest to the Ninth is the Fourth, because both works begin with the experience of innocence and then fight to regain it. The Fourth accomplishes this humorously, in a visionary finale that captures a childhood dream of paradise. In the Ninth, Mahler has no time for such illusions, finding solace in the embrace of death itself. It's an unflinching vision, not so much bitter or fatalistic as it is simply realistic and unafraid. Indeed, the music's extraordinary emotional directness has earned the Ninth the admiration of many listeners and musicians who do not ordinarily warm to Mahler at all—an interesting fact given its supposedly tough musical message and often advanced harmonic language.

First Movement

The first movement of this symphony is so remarkably of a piece, so organic in shape and structure, that many consider it to be the finest single thing that Mahler ever created. Lasting about twenty-seven to thirty minutes in performance, like so many of his most varied and complex movements, it rests on a foundation of a few easily remembered themes and motives that emerge out of silence hesitantly and with simple dignity (just as the work will ultimately end). The thematic exposition for the entire movement takes only about the first five minutes. The rest is all development.

The most important short motives, all of which appear in the first few seconds, are:

1 a faltering rhythm of three notes in the cellos and horn
2. a four-note bell motive on the low strings of the harp
3. a five-note thematic fragment on the acid tones of the stopped horn

The two main tunes, which follow immediately, include:

Theme I: A gentle strain in broken phrases beginning with two falling two-note sequences

Note the resemblance between this music and the ending of *Das Lied von der Erde,* where this music belongs to the word *ewig.* As so often happens in Mahler, the latest symphony takes up the argument where the previous one left it.

The music exudes sweet nostalgia, and it's worth mentioning that Mahler gives this tune, as well as several others in the symphony, to the second violins alone on its first appearance. This melody slowly unfolds, taking its time, accompanied by gentle rustlings in the shape of the bell motive and constant repetitions of the descending two-note figure with which it began. The mood darkens as a solo horn takes over the two-note figure, leading to a dramatic thud on the timpani and a dark chord on the trombones, ushering in:

Theme 2: A quicker, contrasting minor key theme in the violins that's a mirror image of the opening

While that tune gave the impression of descent, this one is all upward-striving. The general shape of its initial phrases, in fact, proclaims it as belonging to the family of motives that I call Mahler's aspiration theme: a descent followed by a rising scale, often repeated and rising successively higher at each stage in the ongoing sequence. Notice that the horns continue with the descending two-note phrases during this theme as well.

This thrusting passage rises quickly to a despairing climax on the horns, but the violins regroup and carry the music into a trumpet fanfare featuring a prominent example of the Mahler rhythm, and with a huge crescendo on the timpani, the music comes round full circle to an ecstatic, *fortissimo* statement of the opening theme in the violins, underpinned by the four-note bell motive in the horns and the five-note motive, now on solo trumpet. Mahler takes the time to expand the broad flow of melody in new directions, and it finally comes to rest in a series of descending two-note phrases. The remainder of the movement consists of developments of this material; these developments come in three huge waves, each ending

in a successively more devastating collapse and return to the
motives of the introduction.

Wave 1 (approximately four minutes)

Mahler begins with theme 2 and immediately tosses in the
fanfare with the Mahler rhythm. This rises rapidly to a pair of
cymbal-capped climaxes, leading to a triumphant fanfare for
the entire brass section over a crescendo on suspended cymbals
and a huge timpani roll that obliterates all sense of the music's
victorious progress. As the timpani subside, horns intone the
three-note opening rhythm, and a second set of timpani thumps
out the bell motive. Stopped horns (their buzzing tone colors
this entire movement) comment with threatening fanfares in
the Mahler rhythm, as the opening motives pass to trumpets
(the bell motive) and trombones (the rhythm).

More stopped horns lead to muted trombones blaring out the
descending two-note phrase, with a sinister tam-tam stroke on
each second note. A wandering cello tune drifts in, accompanied by solo harp intoning what begins as the bell motive and
soon turns into a steadily rising figure, always in four notes so
that its derivation remains clear. The mood gradually lightens,
horns play the descending two-note motive as at the beginning
of the symphony, and Mahler softly begins:

Wave 2 (approximately seven minutes)

The opening theme returns in the winds as a counterpoint to
a new theme on the violins, a tune that actually comes from a
Strauss waltz called *Freuet euch des Lebens* (Enjoy Life). Played
quietly, in a slow tempo, it has a hypnotic, fragile beauty that
simply can't last. And it doesn't. Trumpets sound a distant fanfare, echoed by the timpani in a menacing crescendo, and the

music charges into battle. Timpani pound out the bell motive and violins take over the five-note horn motive. Against these reiterations of familiar music, the brass interject descending fanfares, until finally, with a mighty crash on the cymbals, the entire orchestra comes together and the bottom drops out from below like the opening of a trap door, as over another suspended cymbal crescendo the music collapses into the abyss, landing with a thud on rolling timpani—one of Mahler's classic climaxes gone wrong.

Theme 1 having failed to achieve its objective, theme 2 now has a try. As the orchestra regroups in a remarkable passage of upwardly groping fragments, the strings begin a roiling contrapuntal episode, often in six independent parts, all based on the darkly passionate second theme. Horns add commentary at important climaxes, but this brief storm rapidly exhausts itself, having achieved nothing. Once again the music returns to square one. Muted trombones and tuba utter a mournful version of the trumpet fanfare with the Mahler rhythm, while stopped and normal horns play theme 1's two-note descending phrase, stretching it out to painful lengths. Slowly the orchestra begins to emerge from the darkness as rustling strings begin a steady upward climb against the two-note phrases in the horns.

Wave 3 (approximately four minutes)

This begins with the same music as wave 2, differently orchestrated. Two solo violins take up the Strauss waltz while flutes and clarinets have bits of theme 1. The music gains in confidence, the tempo picks up, and the violins launch the third and final attempt to vanquish the powers of darkness. The full orchestra enters with solo trumpet in the lead, and fanfare figures featuring the Mahler rhythm combined with the bell motive eventually achieve a climax propelled by a bass drum roll leading to a cymbal crash. But this isn't sufficient, and Mahler urges the orchestra on to an even greater climax, led by the trumpet and violins playing a five-note melodic turn (remember that detail!) with even louder support from bass drum and cymbals. But this climax too goes wrong, and the orchestra quite literally plummets over the cliff, rushing downwards in a torrent of trumpet and descending strings and striking the ground with an explosive crash on tam-tam and bass drum.

Trombones and tuba blast out the symphony's opening rhythm "with the utmost power," and timpani pound out the bell motive. As the violence subsides to abrupt reiterations of the bell motive in the brass over quiet tam-tam strokes, the muted trumpets initiate the very last of Mahler's funeral marches. Under the timpani's reiterations of the bell motive, violins and muted trumpets exchange fanfares, leading at last to the bell motive finally played, as was its destiny, on consoling low-pitched chimes. It's amazing, the range of moods and colors that Mahler wrings from these four notes.

The remaining third of the movement (about nine minutes) constitutes a reaction to the previous catastrophe. Theme 1 returns, but as it gains in strength it becomes increasingly deformed, staggering drunkenly into theme 2's despairing climax, its innocence seemingly lost forever. Suddenly the tension evaporates, and Mahler treats his listeners to a ghostly passage of orchestral chamber music, scored primarily for piccolo, flute, clarinet, horn, and just a handful of lower strings (very much like the similar passage at the end of the Seventh Symphony's "Nachtmusik I"). This has the effect of exorcising any remaining angst, and it leads to a small climax, capped by a hopeful roll on the triangle. As the music subsides, the horns, supported by the harp, gently intone the trumpet fanfare with Mahler rhythm, all sense of struggle gone. Ever so gradually, after an ethereal flute solo, a single violin steals back in with the Strauss waltz tune, and then horns and strings take turns repeating those descending two notes, over and over, until the music evaporates into thin air. The last sound heard comes from the piccolo and cellos playing as softly as possible.

Second Movement

The second movement alternates three dances in three different tempos and has the following pattern: ABaBCaCBCABA. Little *a* means that the music of the first dance appears briefly in the middle of B and C when they first appear, serving as a point of contrast. Here's a brief look at each section in order of appearance, paying particular attention to those factors that place this scherzo within the musical orbit of the first movement.

Dance A

This is a deliberately clunky and crude country dance with string drones reminiscent of the sound of bagpipes. Simple rising scales on violas and bassoons lead to three clarinets and bass clarinet playing a humorous but clearly audible variation of the first movement's descending two-note motive. This becomes especially clear when the horns take over the tune, as they just played the same motive a minute ago. Also as in the first movement, Mahler scores the main theme in the strings for the second violin section, and it's many bars (forty-nine of them to be exact) before the first violins have anything at all to contribute.

Dance B

This is a drunken waltz in quicker tempo (and it gets faster each time it reappears), with prominent Mahler rhythms. It contains a rude "parody of a parody" when dance A shows up in the faster tempo for a couple of minutes and has a hilariously difficult time keeping up with its more rapid cousin. Like the first dance, however, the melody consists of a descending chain of sequences containing only two pitches, and thus represents a variation on the first movement's theme 1, now followed in the next phrase by that melodic turn that appeared at the first movement's big climax. This waltz doesn't want to end; it leads to a vulgar circus tune on trombones and tuba and continues with thumping timpani, becoming increasingly raucous until low brass apply the brakes in a series of flatulent blasts that successfully reduce the energy level in preparation for:

Dance C

This slow dance most closely resembles the first movement's theme 1, as it begins with exactly the same descending two-note phrase twice repeated. Dance A interrupts on woodwinds and triangle, offering a mocking commentary. This gracious dance hasn't much of a chance in this company. Dance B returns, more wild than ever, with cymbals, triangle, and glockenspiel added for emphasis, and the brass need assistance from the bass drum to rein it in this time around. Dance C now returns, but it hasn't the energy to resist the return of dance A, more thinly scored (for a husky solo viola) and now marred by darkly ironic commentary from the oboes.

Once again dance B mischievously steals onto the scene. The low brass try to prevent its return with their rude blasts, but it's all in vain. To pounding timpani, the circus tune erupts in the violins, and the waltz swirls through the orchestra with ever-increasing wildness. A solo trumpet finally calls a halt, and with a marvelously graphic musical equivalent of a sneer, horns, then trombones, then tuba call it quits. Dance A returns, its rustic good spirits now constantly undermined by sinister interjections. As the coda begins (to ominous timpani strokes), the contrabassoon has a grotesque solo, and like the scherzos of the Sixth and Seventh Symphonies, the music gradually falls apart into scattered fragments. At the very end, the music recaptures something of its original good cheer, until piccolo and contrabassoon blow the whole thing away with an ironic shrug.

Third Movement

Mahler calls this exercise in musical hostility "Rondo: Burleske." The elements of bitterness and parody speak for themselves, but the form calls for some comment. A rondo is a verse and refrain form having the structure ABACA, etc. (there's no effective limit to the number of sections). In musical parlance, A is called the ritornello, while the alternating sections are called episodes. Mahler has a very good time with this form in the finales of the Fifth and Seventh Symphonies, and he created some of the most complex and funny examples of it. Here the comedy takes a darker turn. The basic form of this movement is ABABACA, but as you will see, the episodes B and C aren't merely individual themes, but extensively developed sections with many diverse components.

The rondo's principal theme—A, or ritornello—is actually a fierce section of jagged counterpoint, with motives tossed among brass, strings, and woodwinds. Trumpets and strings open the movement in a manner very close to that of the Fifth Symphony's similarly stormy second movement, and the music takes off like a bat out of hell. The entry of the triangle signals the beginning of the first episode (B), at the same tempo but in a major key. Just as contrapuntally busy, these new tunes offer a cheerful contrast to what has come before, but Mahler rudely interrupts the party with a loud cymbal crash and an even more violent version of the opening ritornello (as always with Mahler, repetitions are never literal). Note the rising scale on tuba underpinned by thuds on the bass drum, which adds to the atmosphere of ominous clowning.

Once again the triangle leads to a new episode (modified B), this time enriched by glockenspiel. The music consists partially of motives from the first episode and partially of new material, including a parody on the horns of the happy march from the first movement of the Third Symphony (accompanied by pointed *dings* on triangle and glockenspiel). The ritornello returns again on lower strings as a counterpoint to a loud theme announced on the unison horns. Violins answer *fortissimo* with a sour tune beginning with a little five-note melodic turn. It passes in a flash and you may miss it, but it's about to become very important, because as the texture starts to thin, the music seems to recede into the distance, and with another sudden cymbal crash, the mood changes completely, and we find ourselves in an entirely new, slow episode (C).

Here lies this movement's attempt to find a haven of peace and tranquility. Under a quiet tremolo high in the violins, a solo trumpet plays a motive containing that little five-note melodic turn. This is in fact the same instrument and motive that heralded the climax of the first movement's third wave, just before its biggest collapse. But as you will see, this turns out to be a principal motive not of the first movement but of the finale to come. Strings take up this melody, and in a series of lyrical stages, it develops into a passionate and sincere expression of warmth and sentiment. This comes to a full close, followed by a gentle coda in the woodwinds.

A sudden blast on stopped horns, muted trombones and tuba, and a dark timpani roll lead to a rising harp glissando and a return to the episode's opening stillness. But instead of the tender trumpet solo, a quartet of meanspirited clarinets takes the trumpet's motive and spits it out to the accompaniment of malicious chuckles in the flutes. The harp tries again, and the ominous music of the ritornello erupts in the brass, followed again by the mocking clarinets. Once again the harp, leading to the ritornello; and yet again—now the oboe tries the trumpet theme in its original form, but the clarinets answer with the main theme of the ritornello. One last effort by the harp, and the trumpet finally recaptures its original mood, but when the strings take it up, their climax collapses in exhaustion.

As the strings mutter snatches of the trumpet tune, the music of the ritornello steals in quietly. A sudden summons in the brass, and the full ritornello (A) explodes on the trombones, capped by cackling winds and lunatic glockenspiel, as if the entire orchestra has suddenly gone mad. The remainder of the movement needs little comment: it consists of a coda based on the music of the ritornello repeated over and over, getting faster and faster, scored with ever-greater brilliance and hostility, until at last screaming woodwinds, percussion, and lacerating strings slam the movement to a close with the same music that launched it. A more graphic illustration of malicious anger it would be difficult to imagine.

Fourth Movement

Mahler hasn't ended a symphony with an adagio slow movement since the finale of the Third, but the Ninth is by no means a finale symphony. Movements two through four are all reactions to the dramatic events that precede them, and there's nothing at all unusual in that. Classical-period practice most often dictates that the first movement of a symphony is the largest and most formally sophisticated, and the problem for Mahler doesn't lie in writing a bigger last movement, but rather in making his finale sound inevitable, the only possible conclusion irrespective of its relative size and formal complexity. He does this in several ways.

This adagio has a comparatively simple form: ABABABA–coda. Each repeat is both varied and more extended than the previous one and so gives the impression of both a return to and a development of earlier material.

Section A opens with a clear reference to the third movement's trumpet melody (with that melodic turn), which, as you have seen, actually made the briefest of appearances at the climax of the first movement. Then the strings begin a hymn-like theme with several interesting features, not the least of which is the prominent role given the Mahler rhythm, as well as the fact that this tune is actually a very slow transformation of the second-movement waltz. You probably won't hear this consciously, and I don't think Mahler intended that you should. But what you will hear is that this hymn contains the same descending phrases followed by the melodic turn, and so also derives from the first movement's theme 1. Notice how that turn has progressively infected the symphony, appearing just once in the first movement, a bit more in the second movement, still more prominently in the Rondo: Burleske, and now as perhaps the most important motive in the finale.

At two extended points, the string music yields to B, an interlude featuring a rising phrase, first on bassoon, then on the even darker contrabassoon. This interlude first appears briefly before being swamped by a return of the string hymn, a classic case of Mahler's anticipation technique such as was seen in the first movements of the Second and Third Symphonies, the Andante of the Sixth, and elsewhere. But here's the important thing: this hopeless, passionless (Mahler marks it to be played "without expression") rising idea represents the last appearance in Mahler of his aspiration theme and so derives from theme 2 of the first movement. Of course, the point of using this theme here, in this context, is to demonstrate that there is nothing more worth aspiring to: this is music now empty of purpose, groping blindly towards a dawn that will never come. It's a stunning thematic transformation.

And so Mahler contrives that this finale not only serves as the contrasting partner to the third movement (just as the second movement mirrored the first), it also summarizes and transforms the content of the entire symphony. At its central climax, after three increasingly extended "passionless interludes" (the last of which introduces a rocking figure on harp and clarinets from *Das Lied von der Erde,* like a gently ticking clock), Mahler even brings back the three-note rhythm that opened the symphony, now in a searing passage for massed violins leading to the transcendent return of the movement's opening hymn. But the mood of transfiguration isn't to last. The passion slowly drains from the music, and the texture gradually thins down to solo strings—a single cello muttering the melodic turn and lacking the energy to even finish its phrase.

Second violins (again) introduce the ghostly coda, a written-out experience of death. The music hangs by a thread, stops, starts again, its broken phrases punctuated by pauses that seem to last an eternity. Only the muted strings play; the rest of the orchestra sits silently. This last page of music, so tender and soft that it approaches the threshold of hearing, portrays the moment of death, neither as the prelude to life eternal nor as an object of fear, but as a last opportunity to recapture the simple wonder of living in its most pure and basic form (as the simple opposition between sound and silence). It's both the only possible answer to the questions posed by the opening movement and the only way back to the unfettered innocence with which the symphony began.

Afterword

The Ninth Symphony was not the end, despite the fact that Mahler never completed his Tenth. He died in the spring of 1911, not yet fifty-one years old, at the height of his powers as a composer. In fact, his creative life (as it concerns us here) encompassed only about two decades. Symphonically speaking there is no early Mahler at all, only a mature body of work remarkable for both its range and consistency. Few composers sound so different from one work to the next but paradoxically have such instantly identifiable musical fingerprints. Indeed, taken as a whole, the symphonies increasingly come to look like a single, large piece of music, broken merely for the sake of convenience into individual chunks. This is one of the reasons Mahler's so fascinating, and also so easy to "get into."

I have also tried to suggest some of what lies beneath the music's beguiling surface colors and flamboyant emotional appeal in order to explain, however imperfectly, why Mahler's symphonies are great from a musical perspective, and not to simply accept this as given because they happen to be popular at present. This matters—because if, as I truly believe, they reward as much time as you are willing to give them, the reason must be that there's always something new to discover. It doesn't mean that the music has to be complicated in a way that presents barriers to unsophisticated listeners, but rather that the music has depth and that its length and size, its form, is inseparable from its content and expressive intentions. This is the way of all great art. Mahler knew it, and if I have succeeded at least in part in doing his music justice, you do too.

Appendix 1
That Glorious Mahlerian Orchestra!

L ove him or hate him, few will deny that Mahler was arguably the finest symphonic orchestrator that ever lived. I say
"symphonic" because Mahler's instrumental writing is
more than a model of clarity, color, subtlety, and brilliance. It
actually furthers the line of symphonic development, supports
his music's formal and structural design, and opens the way to
an entirely new world of musical argument and logic that has
had an incalculable impact on twentieth-century music.

As Mahler was a master contrapuntal composer who tended
to think of music polyphonically (that is, as several independent
lines or voices happening at once), you will not find any padding
in his orchestration. Every note, line, instrument, color, plink,
twitter, thud, grunt, swoosh, and screech is meant to be heard.
Mahler's obsession with clarity above all else led him to an
extremely innovative use of a very large orchestra, often so as
to have at his disposal an entire group of "mini-orchestras" vari-
ously constituted to give his melodies and movements maximum
contrast and variety. But rather than continue to talk about it,
let's see Mahler's orchestration operating in practice.

On the accompanying CD, play track 2, where you will
hear Michael Gielen's performance of the first movement of the
Second Symphony. Listen straight through the first 5 minutes
and 50 seconds, after which the development section formally

begins. Now go back and listen again, paying special attention to the cellos and basses. They start the symphony together after the opening violin tremolo. Gradually other instruments join in, but they continue on beneath the surface even after the first big cymbal crash. Violins then enter softly with a new, rising tune, but below them the cellos and basses keep up their obsessive muttering, playing what in effect might be called a single, huge melody for more than five and half minutes! This is one brand of Mahler's counterpoint in action, a river of music passing through a landscape of shifting colors and contours.

Later on, at 7:30, you hear another kind of counterpoint: three distinct planes of sound: (1) the marching cellos and basses, (2) the undulating violins, and (3) the melody in long notes on English horn and bass clarinet. You can focus on each line separately or simply take in the entire sound picture as a unit, but however you choose to listen to Mahler, you will very seldom encounter a passage, no matter how lightly scored, in which almost every instrument or section does not have some independent melody, motive, or idea to contribute.

While some of Mahler's ideas last a very long time, and may even use an unvarying tone color throughout, more often he shows as much concern with keeping the timbres of his melodies fresh and ever-changing as in keeping his textures clear. If you take the beginning of the development section, back at about 5:50, and pay attention this time only to the music's surface, to the tunes, you will hear Mahler pass the theme from violins, to horns, to high woodwinds in various combinations, to trumpets, to English horn, to clarinets, to horns and violins, to cellos, to clarinets again (the soft duet at 6:55), and so on, a genuine kaleidoscope of instrumental color.

This ongoing exploration of the infinite possibilities of the symphony orchestra represents the principal reason that it's difficult to say that Mahler ever really finished any of his symphonies: he revised and tinkered with each one prior to every new performance. His orchestration is not the result of theorizing on paper but rather the result of trial and error, much practical experience, experimentation with acoustics and instrumental placement, and a precise knowledge of what each instrument can and can't do, both singly and in groups.

Mahler's Orchestra Section by Section

Strings

Perhaps the most interesting thing about Mahler's vision of the string section lies in what he does not say about it. Both Wagner and Strauss were extremely specific and gave exact numbers for violins, violas, cellos, and basses. Mahler never does. He simply asks that strings be "as numerous as possible" most of the time, while also adding that the basses should have a little gadget attached that permits them to play all the way down to a very low C. This tells us two things about Mahler: first, that he was above all being practical. He knew (even truer in his time than in ours) that no standard-sized string section existed, and as always, he was more concerned with questions of balance and transparency than with sheer numbers.

Second, the role of the strings in the Mahlerian orchestra is not the starring one that it is with Wagner, Strauss, and most other composers (although the strings become more important in the later works than in the earlier ones). Indeed, with the exception of the Sixth, the most classical of all of Mahler's symphonies, not a single work begins with a melody played primarily by the first violins. This is a remarkable fact, when you think about it.

This isn't to say that Mahler underutilizes his violin section. Indeed, he makes it do things that no string section had been asked to do before, particularly in the area of percussive effects. He's very fond of having his players tap the strings with the back of their bows (col legno or "with the wood"), producing a dry clicking sound. As an adjunct to this effect, Mahler invented a technique that translates into English as "stuck with the bow," which basically means that the player should slap the string hard enough so that the hair of the bow rebounds against the wooden stick. In the first movement of the Second Symphony, you can hear the whole string section whacking away (at 14:08), cutting clearly through the texture, despite the fact that brass and percussion are going crazy at the same time.

But of all the things that Mahler does with and to his string players, no effect is more important that the related techniques of portamento and glissando. The first means "leaning" from one note to the next (a clear slide off the note in the direction of the one following), while the second term means "slide from one note to the other, including all the notes in between." The difference between the two terms as Mahler uses them is largely technical and unimportant. Suffice it to say that sometimes it's possible to execute a genuine glissando, at others portamento will do, but in all cases Mahler specifies every instance where he wants it to happen, adding footnotes and other marginalia as necessary. Overindulgence in this effect can make the music sound soupy, sentimental, and cheap, which is often exactly the effect that Mahler wants.

But at other times, as at 17:28 in the first movement of the Second Symphony, where you can hear the glissandos quite clearly in the violins, the impression is one of gentle nostalgia, sweetness, and bittersweet longing. As with all of Mahler's special effects, the degree to which the players honor his requests varies tremendously from orchestra to orchestra and from conductor to conductor. One of the acid tests of any Mahler performance is the willingness of the players to make a rough, crude, sleazy, tacky, or ugly sound, and nowhere does he encounter more resistance in this respect than from an orchestra's string section.

Finally, a word on the harp. Mahler can correctly be said to have discovered the harp as a melody instrument, and in this connection, he was the first composer to find a poetic use for the instrument's bell-like low notes. These open the Ninth Symphony, for example, and close the Fourth. In the first movement of the Second Symphony, you can hear them tolling gently in transition to the beginning of the development section (from 5:40 on). In his larger symphonies, such as the Second, Third, Sixth, and Eighth, Mahler clearly wants as many harps as possible, but four at a minimum. You will almost never see more than two in performance, generally for financial reasons. On those rare occasions when Mahler does get what he requires, you will be amazed at how well the sound of the massed harps stands against that of the full orchestra, even at the loudest moments.

Brass

As with the strings, Mahler's treatment of the brass is as interesting for what he does not do as for what he does. No matter how many trumpets, horns, and trombones he may call for, Mahler never in his life used more than a single tuba in any of his symphonies. The reason for this is that multiple tubas only produce muddy, indistinct textures, and having several of them playing in unison does not enhance the clarity of the bass line.

This doesn't, however, mean that Mahler neglected the possibilities of the tuba. In fact, he emancipated that instrument from being a mere bottom for the trombones. His symphonies abound in solos, most notably at the beginning of the finale of the Sixth and in the Scherzo (third movement) of the Seventh.

When it comes to the other members of the brass family, Mahler's writing is as freewheeling as it gets. All of the symphonies feature lyrical solos for the trumpet, a habit partly the legacy of his childhood near the barracks, partly a gift of Italian opera where the trumpets often double the singer, and partly a result of Mahler's deliberate effort to get away from the strings as the guys who always get to play the tune. The Third, Fifth, and Seventh Symphonies, as well as *Das Lied von der Erde,* all open with brass solos.

In terms of numbers, Mahler greatly multiplied the quantity of brass players in his orchestras. The normal classical or romantic orchestra requires two trumpets. In his Second Symphony, Mahler asks for ten, and four to six is more like the norm for him. Trombone sections traditionally come in threes, but Mahler tends to like four, with additional ones offstage as needed. The standard four-man horn section appears in Symphonies No. 4, 7, 9, and *Das Lied.* Otherwise Mahler requires anywhere from six to ten, and his symphonies are full of rewarding horn solos (especially in the gigantic Scherzo of the Fifth, where the principal horn is so important that he or she sometimes comes to the front of the stage and plays standing, like a concert violinist). Mahler's horn writing in general partakes of the great German romantic tradition extending back through Wagner to Carl Maria von Weber, whose music Mahler adored—even to the point of finishing an incomplete opera: *Die Drei Pintos* (a delightful, too-little-known work with as much Mahler in it as Weber).

Mahler expects all of his brass players to use mutes where required. This practice is deceptive. Mutes do not necessarily make brass instruments sound softer; they change the quality of the tone to something nasal and rasping. He's also careful to distinguish between muted horns, which really are softer, and "stopped tones," in which the player sticks his or her fist into the bell of the instrument to create a harsh buzzing sound. If you want to hear how effective this acid sonority can be, check out the opening movement of the Second Symphony from 1:10 onwards to the big cymbal crash. Another advantage to all of these muted and squeezed notes is that they don't cover other instruments, but rather set their tone into higher relief. This allows Mahler to contrive full, fascinating accompaniments using lots of players and instruments without ever obscuring the principal melody.

Most importantly, Mahler's brass instruments play fanfares, tattoos, military signals, and calls to arms. The fanfare is a constant in Mahler, and you hear them loud, soft, onstage, off-stage, echoed in other instruments, muted, unmuted, joyous, threatening, dreamy, and nostalgic. Just as the Mahlerian finger-print in the strings is portamento/glissando, for the brass it's the fanfare. In the first movement of the Second Symphony, check out the explosion at 9:50, where you can practically see the trumpets shouting "Charge!" as they crash forward (and note their two little muted calls as the noise fades away). The central climax of the movement (from about 13:20 onwards) consists largely of a series of fanfares, on trumpets, timpani, woodwinds, horns, and finally the entire orchestra, as it grinds onward to the recapitulation and the return of the opening theme in the cellos and basses.

Woodwinds

The woodwind section is in some ways the heart and soul of the Mahlerian orchestra, for the simple reason that the woodwinds are the orchestral comedians. They also provide the sounds of nature, of birds, and they combine the agility of the strings with the penetrating power of the brass—that is, when used in sufficient numbers. Mahler's symphonies use more wind players on average than anyone else's. The standard orchestra employs woodwinds (flutes, oboes, clarinets, and bassoons) in pairs. With Mahler, four is closer to the usual number for each instrumental type, and it's the traditional extras (piccolos, English horns, E-flat and bass clarinets, and contrabassoons) that often occur in pairs. To gain even more volume at big moments, Mahler often requests that the oboes and clarinets play with their bells up, pointing the mouth of the instrument directly at the audience and blasting away. Mahlerians in the know always check at this point to see if the conductor and his or her players follow Mahler's instructions: it's a good indication of their commitment to the cause.

Whether humorous, spiteful, sarcastic, or ironic, woodwinds dominate Mahler's scherzos: witness the drunken clarinets in the Second Symphony, the bird and animal imitations in the Third, the vicious cackling and awkward games in the Sixth, and the clunky peasant dances in the Ninth (second movement). Elsewhere, Mahler uses his woodwind section the way an editor uses one of those yellow highlighters. They give a bold, hard edge to his melodic lines, a sharp tang to the upper notes of the violins, and an extra cut and thrust to lower strings and brass. He delights in their shrillness. Listen to the wind entrances at the opening of the Second Symphony (including the passage with stopped horns at 1:10 noted above), and notice how they hold their own against the strings and brass as the first climax arrives.

If the Mahlerian fingerprint for the strings is the portamento/glissando, and for the brass it is the fanfare, then for the winds it is the trill, or *shake* as it's sometimes called. Mahler loves to include this nose-thumbing gesture in so many of his quicker melodies, or as a burbling and subversive accompaniment to a tune on other instruments singing above it. A classic passage illustrating this point occurs in the second movement of the Seventh Symphony, just after the opening horn calls (CD Track 4, at 0:33). The entire wind section builds a huge crescendo (culminating in a scream, I might add), consisting of chattering trills, like a swarm of buzzing insects. And yet the trill can also be glorious, as when piccolos and flutes decorate majestic horn fanfares in the finale of the Second Symphony. With every such gesture in Mahler, if it has more than one meaning, you can be sure that he knows them all and uses them accordingly.

Percussion

Mahler was acknowledged even in his own lifetime as a pioneer in the use of percussion instruments, although this was not necessarily regarded as a compliment. Until he came along, the triangle was the only percussion instrument aside from timpani with an accepted place in the German symphonic orchestra, and then only rarely. Bass drum, cymbals, and triangle were known as "Turkish" instruments and reserved for music descriptive of exotic locales or battle marches (as in Beethoven's Ninth or Haydn's "Military" Symphony).

In Mahler's day, extensive use of percussion was considered in poor taste and incompatible with the German symphonic style. In Russia, composers like Tchaikovsky and Rimsky-Korsakov were doing wonderful things with large percussion sections (although not in symphonies), while Liszt, the inventor of the symphonic poem, similarly had no such inhibitions. But even Wagner (the archrevolutionary of late romantic German music) remained very conservative in his use of percussion, despite important innovations in so many other areas of orchestral practice.

Mahler, for his part, couldn't have cared less about such theoretical notions of musical purity. His goal was to use every expressive means at his disposal, and one of the most significant ways in which he enriched the vocabulary of orchestral music was through his creative use of musical gestures: a single chord, a rhythm, a crash, a scream, or a thud. Many of these simple sounds involve percussion, and entire symphonies can take their characteristic color from them. Examples include the sleigh bells that open the Fourth, the cowbells in the Sixth, and the quiet tam-tam strokes that always accompany Mahler's funeral marches.

So Mahler's percussion writing is not decoration: it is necessary to the symphonic argument and serves a real structural purpose. Listen carefully to the quiet gong beats underpinning the trudging cellos and basses from 4:40 in the Second Symphony's first movement, and to the even more ghostly return of the same music from 18:45. Understanding musical form involves your memory, and every time after this that you hear a soft stroke on the tam-tam, you will remember that first time, whether or not the rest of the music that accompanied the initial sound returns. This is one important way that Mahler binds his movements together—using simple tone colors as mnemonic cues.

Here is the complete list of percussion instruments (aside from timpani) that Mahler asks for at one time or another in his symphonies: triangle, crash cymbals, suspended cymbals, bass drum, bass drum with cymbal attached, mallet glockenspiel, keyboard glockenspiel, high tam-tam, standard tam-tam, low tam-tam, piano, celesta, snare drum, slapstick, rute (bundle of sticks beaten on the bass drum case), a small wooden stick (also tapped on the bass drum case), military parade drum, hammer, cowbells, steel bars, deep bells, tubular chimes, tambourine, xylophone, and sleigh bells.

On average, Mahler requires from three to five extra players to handle his percussion parts, and there's always a lot of running around as well: onstage and offstage, extra hands needed for isolated timpani strokes, or cymbal crashes, or exotica such as cowbells.

It's impossible to exaggerate just how radical Mahler's approach was musically (wider cultural issues aside) at a time when the quality of most percussion sections, in German orchestras especially, was simply terrible. He would travel from one performance of his music to the next with his own percussion section in tow, even scheduling special rehearsals for the percussionists alone simply to explain to the players what he was trying to achieve. In all of this he was regarded as very eccentric.

Wagner used two pairs of timpani in his "Ring" operas. Mahler often uses two sets, usually of three to four drums each, and like Berlioz, he is careful to specify which type of mallet the players should use: soft-headed sticks or hard, wooden ones (he also asks for mutes on more than one occasion). He was one of the first composers to write for timpani melodically: the kettledrums actually get the tune in the third movement of the Second Symphony and the first movement of the Fifth, and they always participate fully in the symphonic development of themes and motives, especially in the Sixth, Seventh, Eighth, and Ninth Symphonies. Every symphony without exception includes important timpani solos, and Mahler expects the players to have at their disposal a range of notes so wide that special instruments have been constructed simply to play them accurately.

I suggest that you listen to the passage in the first movement of the Second Symphony beginning at 11:00. In the space of a few seconds, you hear: (1) woodwinds accompanied by triangle, (2) a solo bass drum beating ominously (the Mahlerian thud), (3) the opening gesture of the cellos and basses separated by two Mahlerian crashes, one for high tam-tam with timpani, the other for low tam-tam with bass drum, (4) the Mahler rhythm (*dum dadum*), hammered out by solo timpani, first loudly and then softly echoed, while the strings play an acid tremolo "on the bridge" of their instruments over a soft roll on the low tam-tam and bass drum.

Here, in some thirty seconds, you can hear everything that makes Mahler's orchestration so special. It's a passage of pure symphonic development; there's no fat, or gratuitous wash of color for its own sake. Every detail amplifies or elaborates something that we have heard before and reveals it in a new light. In the space of ten bars the dynamics go from triple forte (*fff*) to quadruple piano (*pppp*). Believe me when I tell you that no one achieved this sort of meaningful deployment of percussion timbre in the service of musical logic until Mahler found a way to incorporate a vocabulary of simple musical gestures and noises into the flow of symphonic development. And this is what distinguishes Mahler's orchestral writing in general from that of so many others: every note of it contributes to the music's expressive purpose and helps to clarify its formal progress.

Appendix 2
The Symphonies at a Glance

I t may not be possible to reduce any complex piece of music to a mere table or chart, but one of the most interesting thing about Mahler is that he used musical gestures—simple sounds, noises, stylistic archetypes, or even instrumental colors (timbre)—as a method of characterizing his symphonic movements and a means of binding them together. The first three tables below summarize some of these gestures and tell you where you will find them. "Marches and Dances" pretty much speaks for itself; "Screams, Crashes, and Thuds" includes some of the repertoire of dramatic sound effects—bass drum thuds, tam-tam crashes, and instrumental screams—that color Mahler's special sound world. The aspiration or redemption theme is a motive that runs though almost all of Mahler's work, appearing in different contexts. All of these ideas are described in the individual essays at the appropriate points.

The last two tables summarize two separate characteristics. Table 4 tells you where you will find humor, perhaps the least well appreciated quality of classical music in general, and of Mahler in particular. It colors more of his music than you might at first think. Not all of this humor is happy. Sometimes it's bitter or ironic, but either way, it's an expressive fact even more outstanding (if perhaps less obvious) than the sorrow and neurotic despair that seem to monopolize most of the attention when the expressive range of Mahler's music generally comes up for discussion. Finally, table 5 shows you just how varied Mahler's symphonies are in their arrangement of movements and how these movements are grouped to create formal balance and always new answers to questions of large-scale symphonic structure.

Table 1
Marches and Dances

Symphony No.	Waltz/Ländler/Minuet Movement No(s)	March Movement No(s)
1	2	3
2	2 and 3	1 and 5
3	2 and 3	1
4	2 and 3	1
5	3	1 and 2
6	2 (if Scherzo 2nd)	1 and 4
7	3	1 and 2
8	0	1
Das Lied von der Erde	0	4 and 6
9	2	1 and 3
10	2 and 4	0

Table 2
Screams, Crashes, and Thuds

Symphony No.	Scream Movement No(s)	Crash Movement No(s)	Thud Movement No(s)
1	4	4	1 and 3
2	3 and 5	5	1 and 3
3	1 and 3	1	1
4	1, 2 and 3	1 and 3	2 and 3
5	1 and 2	2	1, 2 and 5
6	1, 3 and 4	Scherzo and 4	Scherzo and 4
7	2 and 3	5	3
8	0	1 and 2	0
Das Lied von der Erde	1	1	1 and 6
9	3 and 4	1	1 and 2
10	1 and 5	5	3

Table 3
Appearances of the "Aspiration" or "Redemption" Theme

Symphony No.	Movement No(s)
1	n/a
2	5
3	1 and 4
4	3
5	4 and 5
6	4
7	5
8	1 and 2
Das Lied von der Erde	n/a
9	1 and 4

Table 4
Mahlerian Humor

Symphony No.	Irony/Parody Movement No(s)	Wit Movement No(s)
I	3	I
2	3	2
3	I, 5	3
4	2	I, 3, 4
5		3, 5
6	2	
7	2, 3	4, 5
8		
Das Lied von der Erde	5	3,4
9	2,3	

Table 5
Large-scale Structure

Symphony No.	No. of Movements	Order[a] (f=fast, s=slow)	Focus
I	4 (orig. 5)[b]	f, (s), f,s,f	finale
2	5	f,s,f,s,f	finale
3	6	[f],[sfsfs]	first movement
4	4	f,f,s,f	third movement
5	5	[sf],f,[sf]	third movement
6	4	f,f,s,f (or f,s,f,f)	finale
7	5	f,s,f,s,f	first movement
8	2	[f],[sfsf]	first movement
Das Lied von der Erde	6	[fsfsf],[s]	finale
9	4	s,f,f,s	first movement
I0	5	s,f,f,f,s	finale

a. Movements in brackets [ ] indicate Mahler's division in parts or, in the case of *Das Lied von der Erde*, my own suggestion in keeping with Mahler's practice.

b. Symphony No. I's original second movement was later eliminated.

CD Track Listing

All performances on the enclosed CD are by the SWR Symphony Orchestra of Baden-Baden and Freiburg, conducted by Michael Gielen. Recordings are from the Hänssler Classic CD *Symphonies No. 1–9 and Adagio* by Gustav Mahler (93.130, Ⓟ 2004).

1. Symphony No. 1, Third Movement   (9:49)
2. Symphony No. 2, First Movement   (22:27)
3. Symphony No. 5, Third Movement   (16:25)
4. Symphony No. 7, Second Movement   (16:46)
   ("Nachtmusik I")

Recordings licensed under permission of Hänssler Classic, Max-Eyth-Str.41, D-71088 Holzgerlingen, Germany. All rights reserved.